A

GOSSIP'S STORY,

AND

A .LEGENDARY TALE.

BY THE AUTHOR OF

A DVANTAGES ·OF EDUCATION.

" Nor Peace nor Eafe the Heart can know,
" Which, like the Needle true,
" Turns at the touch of Joy and Woe,
" Yet, turning, trembles too."

GREVILLE'S ODE TO INDIFFERENCE.

IN TWO VOLUMES.

VOL. I.

THE THIRD EDITION.

LONDON:

PRINTED FOR T. N. LONGMAN, PATER-NOSTER-ROW.

1798.

THE following pages intended, under the difguife of an artlefs Hiftory, to illuftrate the Advantages of CONSISTENCY, FORTITUDE, and the DOMESTIC VIRTUES; and to expofe to ridicule, CAPRICE, AFFECTED SENSIBILITY, and an IDLE CENSORIOUS HUMOUR; are moft refpectfully infcribed to

THE HON. MRS, COCKAYNE;

by one who has been long honoured by her friendfhip, who fincerely admires the maternal and conjugal duties exemplified in her conduct; and who wifhes, by her example, to recommend them to others.

CONTENTS

OF THE

FIRST VOLUME.

A 4

V. Female

Rodolpho,

INTRODUCTION.

M RS. Prudentia Homefpun is infinitely ob-
liged to the World, for the favourable reception
it gave to her tale of Maria Williams, or the Advantages of Education ; which more than anfwered her higheft expeɛtations.

The World in reply thanks Mrs. Prudentia for
her politenefs ; but aſſures her, it never heard either of her or her Maria.

Mrs. Prudentia in her rejoinder obferves, that
fhe muft define what thofe expeɛtations were. She
was not romantic enough to imagine, that a little
novel iſſuing from a general repofitory, unfup-
ported by puff, unpatronifed by friends, and even
unacknowledged by its author, could rife into ce-
lebrity. There were befides fome intrinfick reafons why it fhould not fucceed, according to the

A 6   com-

common acceptation of that word. It had no
fplendour of language, no local defcription, nothing of the marvellous, or the enigmatical, no
fudden elevation, and no aftonifhing depreffion.
It merely fpoke of human life as it is, and fo fimple was the ftory, that at the outfet an attentive
reader muft have forboded the cátaftrophe. Indeed it required fome attention from the reader,
which in works of this kind is alfo a fault : for not
ambitious of dazzling the imagination, and of en-
flaming the paffions, it uniformly purfued its aim
of meliorating the temper and the affeɛtions.

No pecuniary advantages, nor the applaufe of
the million could be expeɛted from a work like
this. As to the former, Mrs. Prudentia is happily
too *rich* to wifh for any. Left the word rich
fhould create the idea of a Nabob's fortune, fhe
explains by faying, that fhe poffeffes a clear annuity of one hundred pounds per annum, and that
fhe calls herfelf very wealthy, becaufe it is adequate to all her wifhes.

The

The *general* approbation would not have been sufficient; for the generality of readers do not judge by the rules by which she wishes to be tried. The limited circulation of Maria Williams has afforded her the gratification she desired. She has heard, without fearing any implied flattery, the merit of the work asserted by those, who wondered who could be the author. Many ladies who, by conscientiously discharging the duties of the maternal character, may be presumed to be judges of what is best adapted for the perusal of youth, have commended it, as a work from which much real instruction may be derived. The author's highest expectations presumed upon no further applause.

She has resumed the pen with a similar intention. Happy, if while she is instructing her sex how to avoid yielding to imaginary sorrows, she can, for a moment, banish from her dejected heart, the pressure of *real* calamity, to which it is her duty to submit; or forget the friend whose approbation was the incentive and reward of her *former* labours. Some

Some further apology may be judged neceſſary for introducing a Legendary Tale but ſlightly conneĉted with the principal ſtory. Were this work to be tried by the rules of an epick, the author is ſenſible that the epiſode is conſiderably too long; but ſhe hopes a trifle will not be meaſured upon the bed of Procruſtes. The example of the inimitable Goldſmith, and many later writers, who have ſuccefsfully interſperſed poetry with proſe in works of this nature, excited a wiſh to gratify the publick taſte by ſimilar variety. And as moral improvement is the avowed end, deſcriptive poetry was not thought ſo *impreſſive* as a conneĉted tale, which inſenſibly ran on to a greater length than was at firſt deſigned.

GOSSIP's STORY,

AND

A LEGENDARY TALE.

CHAPTER I.

The comforts of Retirement—Rural Elegance defined by example.

As I profess myself an egotist, it will not be uncharacteristick to begin with stating the qualifications I possess, to execute with propriety the task I have undertaken.

I have been for several years the inhabitant of a small market-town called Danbury, in the north of England. As my annuity is regularly paid, and my family consists of only myself, a female servant, and an old tabby-cat, I have but little domestick care to engage my attention and anxiety. Now, as I am of a very active temper, my mind naturally steps abroad, and occupies itself in the concerns of my neighbours. Besides the peculiar advantages of my situation, I enjoy some inhe-

inherent qualities, which I flatter myfelf
render me a very excellent goffip. I have
a retentive memory, a quick imagination,
ftrong curiofity, and keen perception.
Thefe faculties enable me not only to
retain what I hear, but to conneft the
day dreams of my own mind; to draw
conclufions from fmall premifes; in fhort,
to tell what other people think, as well
as what they do. Other circumftances
alfo confpire to render my pretenfions to
the above charafter indifputable..

As Danbury poffeffes the advantages
of an healthy fituation, dry foil, and pleafant environs, it has long been diftinguifhed for the genteel conneftions which
it affords. Many fingle ladies, like myfelf,
have chofen it for their refidence, and we
have eftablifhed a very agreeable fociety,
which meets three times a week, to communicate the obfervations which the levity
of youth, the vanity of oftentation, or the
meannefs of avarice have fuggefted. Our
                                        remarks

remarks have all the acumen which experience and penetration can fupply, and as we exhibit models of prudence in our own conduct, it is a rule with us to fhew no mercy to others.

I will not attempt to conceal the cenfures which the objects of our animadverfion, in return, affect to throw upon us. I am not ignorant that we are termed the *fcandalous* club, and that fpleen, malevolence, and difappointment are faid to be the idols, on whofe altars we facrifice every reputation which comes within our reach. Perfection belongs to no human inftitution, and I will own that fometimes we *may* be wrong. The reader muft know that I am uncommonly good humoured and tender hearted ; whether therefore my diffent from my lady affociates proceeds altogether from a redundance of " the milk of human kindnefs" in my difpofition, or from too great feverity in theirs, time muft determine.

Amongft the agreeable appendages to Danbury, its vicinity to Stannadine muft be enumerated.

merated. This elegant manfion was. built by a refpectable gentleman, whofe family falling into decay, it has fince become the cafual refidence of feveral genteel people; and has thus been inftrumental in promoting our amufements, not only by its pleafing embellifhments and delightful walks, but by the quick fucceffion of its inhabitants, who fupply a never-failing fource of obfervation and anecdote. I am not going to detail the commodious apartments in the houfe, or to defcribe the grounds, beautiful as they are by nature, and highly cultivated by art. A mere novice in landfcape defignation, I confine myfelf to the delineation of the lights and fhades of human character; and as I conceive the hiftory of the Dudley family may afford inftruction as well as amufement to the younger part of the female world, I fhall dedicate my prefent hiftory to their concerns, hinting at the fame time, that it is not abfolutely impoffible, but that I may at fome future period again treat the publick with fome other delicacy, drawn from the ample ftores I poffefs. No

No fooner was the arrival of Mr. Dudley
and his daughter at Stannadine announced,
than our fociety immediately met, to determine on the propriety of vifiting the ftrangers. This is a preliminary etiquette we have
refolved never to omit in future, fince by a
neglect of circumfpection, we had been betrayed into an intimacy with the laft inhabitants of the manfion, whom we unfortunately
difcovered had amaffed a fortune by keeping
a flop-fhop in Wapping. The univerfal contempt with which we treated them when we
knew their mean origin, had indeed been the
caufe of driving them from the neighbourhood; but as we were all gentlewomen born,
we could not eafily overcome the fecret mortification we had experienced.

We refolved therefore upon the prefent
occafion to be very circumfpect, and exa-
mined in full council all the intelligence
which our refpective Mollies and Betties had
been able to procure from Mr. Dudley's fervants, who had arrived about a fortnight be-

fore

fore to prepare for his reception. Little, I am
forry to fay, could be difcovered. He was juft
come from the Weft-Indies, and had hired
moft of his houfehold in London, it was however gueffed that he was rich, and his efta-
blifhment was upon an expenfive plan.

It was at length determined that we fhould
depute two ladies of our body, in the character of infpeftors, to inform us whether the
Dudleys were *vifitable* beings or not. Mrs.
Medium the Vicar's lady, and Mifs Cardamum the daughter of an eminent medical
gentleman, were felefted for the important
truft. Their abilities were indifputable; as
Mrs. Medium had been for many years an
humble friend to a lady of quality, and Mifs
Cardamum conftantly accompanied her papa
every fummer to Scarborough, it was impoffible they could be impofed upon in the
grand articles of fafhionable appearance and
intrinfick gentility.

It being neceffary, not only to form a
right notion of the Dudleys, but alfo to im-
prefs

prefs them with a high idea of *us*, we determined, though the walk was but half a mile,
and the morning inviting, that Mr. Cardamum's carriage fhould be got ready for the
occafion, and the foot-boy had orders to tie
on his vifiting queue, brufh his livery, and
trim up old Bolus the favourite chair-horfe.
The reins alfo were blacked for the occafion, and all the ornaments of the buggy (I
mean the capriole) furbifhed to the brightnefs of filver. Mifs Cardamum, dreffed in
an elegant new riding habit, was driver ; and
Mrs. Medium, in honour of the embaffy,
was attired in the rich brocade Lady Seraphina gave her on her nuptials, and to take
off from the antiquity of its appearance, fhe
put on a modern hat with three upright feathers. They ftopped at my door, and kindly promifed to give me the firft intelligence of
their return. The fair Belle gave the lafh a
fmart twirl, and Bolus fet off on a good
round trot. Little Joe on Mr. Cardamum's
poney, with his ftick held perpendicular, (as
was

was the fashion amongst the lacquies at Scarborough last season,) followed the carriage as fast as possible.

The result of the visit was communicated in the afternoon, but unhappily the ladies did not agree in their verdict. Miss Cardamum would not assent to Mrs. Medium's determination, that Miss Dudley was handsome and well dressed; and the fair spinster's opinion concerning the elegance of the furniture, and the excellence of the cakes and chocolate, was as warmly disputed by the experienced matron. The points in which they agreed did not tend to inspire us with any very high idea of the strangers. They determined Miss Dudley to be a *shy fearful thing;* Mr. Dudley, on the contrary, had a most intimidating look, which seemed to criticise every word, and to remark every action. A little incident was cited to confirm this observation. Over the chimney was the portrait of a lady, which, when Mrs. Medium admired, and observed how much it put her in mind

of

of one in Lady Seraphina's faloon, Mifs Dudley faid with a figh in a low voice, as if to prevent further inquiry, that it was intended for her mother. She then ftole a timid confufed glance at her father, who withdrew to the window evidently difcompofed. The conclufion which my friends drew from this was, that he had been a fevere hufband, and that his daughter would, if fhe durft, have reproached him for his unkindnefs. I ventured to hint that the fact admitted a contrary inference, but I was preffed fo ftrongly with arguments drawn from Mr. Dudley's ftern manner, and from the reftraint which the poor girl vifibly fuffered, that I was forced to give up my opinion.

After much difcuffion it was at laft agreed, that though they promifed to add but little to the pleafures of Danbury, yet as they certainly were gentlefolks, lived in ftyle, and intended coming to our affembly, we might as well vifit them. And we vifited them accordingly.

CHAP. II.

The Author fhews that fhe ftudies climax, or gradation of Charaƈter.

As it is the duty of all authors to relieve their reader's curiofity as foon as is confiftent with their plans, I fhall dedicate this chapter to introduƈtory ancedotes of the Dudley family, after having made a few preliminary obfervations.

The fpirit of penetration or the ability to difcover people's charaƈters by a curfory glance, though arrogated by almoft every body, is in reality poffeffed by very few. Nothing can be more intricate than the human heart, and the difcriminating fhades which ferve to mark variation of charaƈter, are generally too minute and confufed to write diftinƈt traits upon the countenance. Even words and aƈtions are often deceitful guides. People frequently ftep out of themfelves. The man of fenfe has his weak moments, the

woman

woman of reflection on fome occafions acts inconfiderately. Now though fuch deviations furnifh very agreeable amufement to the cenforious, the idle, and the malevolent; none but the thoughtlefs part of mankind will fee thefe incidental defects in any other light than as a cafual departure from the real character.

I confefs it is my wifh to hunt this faid fpirit of penetration out of the world, as I am convinced it is productive of many ferious evils. It often teaches us to think highly of the unworthy, and meanly of the meritorious. It makes us arrogant and felf opinionated, or elfe expofes us to many difficulties in endeavouring to rectify the erroneous notions we have adopted. It affifts the artifices of falfehood, increafes the allurements of feduction, feathers the fhafts of flattery, and cafts an additional veil over the difguifes of hypocrify. It is one of the errors into which inexperience is moft apt to fall, fpringing from the ingenuous confidence, fanguine paffions, and prompt decifion incident to young minds. Happy are they if they become lefs precipitate in their judgments, before the confequences of their errors are fatal to their peace!

Neither Mrs. Medium nor Mifs Cardamum had the apology of youth or inexperience to plead in excufe for the erroneous conclufions they had drawn. The ladies were arrived at years of maturity, and had been in the courfe of their lives at leaft one thoufand times miftaken. But there are people who never will derive advantages from the paft, who are happy in the art of felf-excufe, and determined to think themfelves always right, who place their own portion of human infirmity to their neighbour's account; and certainly, as they have fo little to do in reforming errors at home, may be allowed to look abroad for employment.

To thofe who prefer fkimming over the fuperficies to diving into the fubftance, ftrong features marked with mafculine fenfe may wear the afpect of ill-humour, and feverity; diffidence will appear like folly; and the

the reserve of polite prudence may be deno-
minated pride. All common observers,
though they love the utmost minuteness in a
story, are fond of difcuffing abftract qualities
in a compendious manner; and I have
known—"Oh, Madam, it was fo foolifh,"
or " She is fo ill-natured," or " Was not that
extravagant," or " He is fo proud," decided-
ly fink a character into fupreme contempt,
even in the fhort period while the fpeaker
was dealing a hand at quadrille. Indeed, ex-
clufive of errors in point of drefs or omif-
fions of ceremonious forms, pride, ill-humour, folly, and extravagance feem to in-
clude all human vices; at leaft in the voca-
bulary of Danbury. One reafon for this
may be that pride and ill-humour wound our
feelings, while the folly and extravagance of
our neighbours are implied compliments to
our own good fenfe and difcretion.

To return to the Dudleys—

Mr. Dudley poffeffed in an eminent degree the virtues of the head and the heart.
Bleffed with the early advantage of a liberal

education, he united the character of the true Gentleman to the no less respectable name of the generous confcientious merchant. Having passed through many viciffitudes of life, he had learned how to form a temperate judgment, and by truly appreciating its pleasures and its pains, he knew how to reduce his defires to that moderate standard, which is moft likely to produce content.

In the death of an amiable wife he had experienced a feverer blow than all the former shocks of fortune could inflict. Two daughters were the offspring of an union, which, while it lafted, produced as much happiness as any fublunary connection could afford. Mrs. Alderfon, the mother of Mrs. Dudley, took the youngeft child immediately upon her daughter's death, with a declared intention of adopting her for her own, and making her heirefs to all her fortune. Louifa, the elder, accompanied her father to Barbadoes, where he had a confiderable eftate, for the improvement of which he judged his prefence abfolutely neceffary.

A mind

A mind like Mr. Dudley's, awakened to
all the impreffions of duty both to his Maker
and his fellow-creatures, muft be fuppofed to
have poffeffed fufficient ftrength to overcome the extreme indulgence of hopelefs
grief. Though he found it impoffible to forget that he was once moft happy, he acquiefced with patient refignation in the limited
enjoyments which his fituation allowed, and
ftifling in his breaft the feelings of widowed
love, endeavoured to fupply its place with the
anxious tendernefs of the paternal character.
Louifa, who from her earlieft years difcovered a difpofition to improve both in moral
and mental excellence, liftened with attention to her father's precepts, illuftrated at
times by the painful yet pleafing defcription
of what her mother was. Inftructions thus
enforced by example, funk with double
weight into her retentive mind ; and fhe early
nurfed the laudable ambition, of copying
thofe amiable virtues, of which her departed
mother and living father exhibited fuch fine
models.   B 2   As

As fhe was at the age of fixteen when fhe
loft her mother, Mr. Dudley's narratives
were ftrengthened by her own recollection.
She had befides the advantage of having
commenced her education under a female
eye, and confequently of acquiring thofe foft
touches of refined elegance, which the moft
experienced male inftructor cannot communicate.

While Louifa thus rofe into woman under
her father's care, in a climate in which
the luxuriant bounty of Nature, and the
fierce contention of the elements, by produ-
cing frequent reverfes of fortune, alternately
excite diffipation and demand fortitude; Marianne experienced under her Grandmother,
all the fond indulgence of doating love. If
ever the exceffes of tendernefs are pardon-
able, they might be in Mrs. Alderfon's circumftances. She had loft an amiable and only
daughter, enchanting as a companion, and
eftimable as a friend; whofe fociety afforded her the greateft delight, whofe conduct
and

and character reflected honour upon herself. It was natural to view the child which her daughter had bequeathed her, with an affection rifing to agonizing fenfibility; to confider it as a pledge from an inhabitant of another world, a relique fnatched from the grave, a bond of union between herself and the glorified fpirit of its immortal mother. Lefs firm than Mr. Dudley, though not lefs attached both to the living and the dead, fhe regarded her Marianne as poffeffing a kind of hereditary claim to perfection, and almoft fuppofed that the neceffity of culture was fuperfeded by the fuperior excellence of the parent plant.

The characters of the young ladies will be fully developed in the enfuing pages, but unwilling to omit any thing which cuftom has rendered neceffary to writers of my clafs, I will fay fomething of their perfonal attractions.

Louifa's figure was tall and elegant, her eyes expreffed intelligence and ingenuous

modefty,

modesty. Her features were more agreeable than beautiful, and her manner, though in general rather placidly reserved than obtrusive or sparkling, was frequently animated by the lively graces of youth. Yet even in those gayer moments her mirth indicated an in-formed, well-regulated mind. Though her education had extended to particulars not usually attended to by females, there was nothing in her conversation to excite the apprehensions which gentlemen are apt to en-tertain of learned ladies. Science in her might be compared to a light placed behind a veil of gauze, which, without being itself apparent, sheds a softened radiance over each surrounding object.

To all who admire beauty in its softest and most feminine dress, Marianne Dudley must have appeared uncommonly attractive. Her features were formed with delicate symmetry, her blue eyes swam in sensibility, and the beautiful transparency of her complexion seemed designed to convey to the admiring beholder

beholder every varying fentiment of her mind. Her looks expreffed what indeed fhe was, tremblingly alive to all the fofter paffions. Though the gentle timidity of her temper had preferved her from the ufual effects of early indulgence, it rendered her peculiarly unfit to encounter even thofe common calamities humanity muft endure. Her natural good health had hitherto preferved her from bodily fufferings; and Mrs. Alderfon had never permitted her to know a forrow which could either be alleviated or removed.

A little time previous to the return of her father and fifter from the Weft Indies, her Grandmother's death rendered her poffeffed of a fortune of fifty thoufand pounds, of which, though only nineteen, it was that Lady's dying requeft fhe fhould be the uncontrolled miftrefs. Thus bleffed with youth, health, beauty, and affluence, what was wanting to render her felicity complete? I doubt not but the younger part of my readers are inclined to think that I fhall defcribe her as *too* happy.   B 5   Mr.

Mr. Dudley, though he had confented from unexceptionable motives to the feparation of his children, ever lamented the circumftance as likely to check the expanfion of the filial and fifterly affections. About the time of Mrs. Alderfon's laft illnefs, difcouraged by the terrible devaftations of a hurricane, he abandoned the fchemes of improvement he had projected upon his eftates, and returning with Louifa into England, offered himfelf to Marianne as her natural guardian and protector. That young lady's heart was too full of fenfibility not to be affected by the manly tendernefs of a father, and the affectionate endearments of a fifter, from whom fhe had been fo long feparated. She readily accepted their invitation to refide with them, and it was with a view to her proper accommodation that Mr. Dudley engaged the fpacious manfion at which in my preceding chapter I announced his arrival. Mifs Marianne was not prefent when my fagacious neighbours decided upon the characters of

the

the Dudleys, having determined to spend a few weeks with an intimate friend, previous to her design of fixing her abode under the paternal roof.

CHAP, III,

A fine instance of modern susceptibility introduces a delicate discussion, which is left to some brighter genius to determine.

FROM this excursive view of characters above the general level, I return with the delight of a bird flying to her nest, to common life, and the dear society in which I spend my hours.

I suppose it was from perceiving even the *voluble spirit* of female conversation droop when unsupported by the presence of gentlemen, that the ancient mythologists constantly grouped Cupid with the Graces, and introduced Apollo into the circle of the Muses. Though the comparison will not perhaps apply in all parts, we ladies of Danbury

в 6   had

had our converfations enlivened by the prefence of a Cupid and an Apollo too, in the
perfons of Captain Target, a militia officer,
firft coufin to a Baronet, a gentleman of unqueftionable honour; and of Mr. Alfop, the
heir of an eminent Attorney, who having
amaffed a confiderable fortune by bufinefs,
educated his fon in what he efteemed the dif-
tinguifhing mark of a gentleman, *Idlenefs*.

Againft thefe Beaux the fair Cardamum
planted all the artillery of love. She long
ago, on examining her own heart upon the
grand queftion, had determined marriage to
be effential to her happinefs; but on advancing to the next point in debate, who fhould
be the man, fhe found herfelf totally unable
to decide, and her heart wandered from one
to the other as local circumftances directed.
Every one knows that the parifh church in
the country anfwers the end of places of
publick refort in London, by giving fafhionable people opportunities of fporting a whim,
making critical obfervations, or attracting
the

the attention of the other fex. I have often feen my fair friend's eyes, even in the moft pathetick parts of Mr. Medium's difcourfe, wander from the Captain's hat, when decorated with the military plume, to Mr. Alfop's fervants in their new liveries, and pitied the perplexities which agitated her gentle bofom. If family, martial addrefs, knowledge of the world, and an infinitude of fmall talk, recommended the accomplifhed Target; no lefs did the charms of youth, wealth, and great docility of temper plead in favour of the rich Alfop. Without pretending to that penetration I decried in a former chapter, it was eafy to difcover the prefent ftate of her heart; as it was an invariable rule to fpeak of the favourite of the week in terms of ftudied contempt or marked cenfure. While her affection rebounded from one gentleman to the other, I was eafy; but when for feveral days together fhe talked of the conceited foppifh airs Target gave himfelf, or of the

pooreft

pooreſt of all poor creatures, Alſop, I trembled for her peace of mind.

The rivals continued to live together in
terms of perfeᴄt intimacy. I muſt ſuppoſe
they were ignorant of the ſtorms they excited
in the breaſt of beauty; for had they known
the ſtate of the lady's heart, could modern
friendſhip have been proof to the temptation
of ſecuring ſo invaluable a prize? I am confirmed in my opinion by reflecting, that extreme humility and ſuperabundant diffidence
are the unhappy failings of the preſent race
of young men. They think too meanly of
themſelves and too exaltedly of us, to dare
to aſpire to the poſſeſſion of the excellence
they at diſtance adore; and though conde-
ſcending ſweetneſs and eaſy acceſs are no leſs
the charaᴄteriſtick of the preſent race of
beauties, their worſhippers are ſo apt to con-
ſider them as inexorable divinities rather than
as placable mortals, that hopeleſs of ſucceſs
they retire from their altars in the dumb
ſilence of deſpair.

But

But I will confider the cafe in another point of view, and propofe a queftion which I hope fome fifter novelift will difcufs, as it is an extremely delicate point of honour, and will bear amplifying through at leaft fifty pages. Suppofing the gentlemen actually perceived the ftate of the lady's heart, could they confiftently with friendfhip and generofity make any efforts to fecure it entirely to themfelves ? Was it not infinitely more congenial to thofe refined principles and delicate diftinctions, invented by feveral French writers, and adopted by our own, to leave her entirely to herfelf, and neither to do any thing tranfcendently praife-worthy, or to fay any thing eminently clever, to influence her decifion ? I cannot determine this point, but will proceed in the narrative way to ftate, that certainly neither of them was guilty of the crime of endeavouring to detain the angel which thus hovered between them.

It would have been a folecifm in good breeding, if Captain Target and Mr. Alfop had

had omitted to pay their devoirs to the Dudley family. The Captain only waited to know whether the cellars were well flocked, and the table hofpitably fupplied, to propofe to his friend a morning walk to Stannadine. Mr. Alfop readily acquiefced in the propofal, though from different motives. Happy as he was in many refpects, he was tormented by the attacks of a cruel invincible enemy, who, in fpite of all his efforts, haunted all his waking hours. This enemy was Time. Such is the ftrange intricacy of human affairs. It was originally beftowed by Providence as an eftimable blefling, an improveable talent, the fource of prefent enjoyment and future felicity.

Full of the heroic defign of killing this monfter, my heroes fallied forth, and were received by Mr. Dudley with politenefs and attention. Captain Target readily fell into converfation; they talked of the Weft-Indies, its important commercial advantages and natural beauties; the military gentleman enlivening the difcourfe with anecdotes of

feveral

several gallant officers, with whom he became acquainted during the summer encampments. Mr. Alsop was silent, contemplating the form of Mr. Dudley's buckles, and wondering if they were more fashionable than his own.

As it was the merchant's custom to banish as much as possible the little rules which etiquette unnecessarily prescribes, the strangers, though it was a first visit, consented to stay dinner, and Mr. Dudley, to employ part of the morning, led them the tour of his pleasure grounds, pointing out some little improvements he proposed to make. To these Captain Target assented with warm approbation, while the modest Alsop, though he equally understood and admired Mr. Dudley's taste, contented himself with the harmless epithets of " vastly pretty, vastly clever indeed."

From the shrubbery they returned to the drawing-room, where Miss Dudley received them with the smile of welcome and the blush blufh of delicacy. Captain Target poured forth a volley of compliments, but could he have attended to any thing but the found of his own voice, he might have perceived that the lady to whom they were addreffed, knew how to eftimate her own worth too well, to be elevated by cafual attentions or fuperficial praife. Mr. Alfop not being fo fluent in his expreffions, contented himfelf with filent admiration, never once withdrawing his eyes from Mifs Dudley, till the fervant fummoned them to the dining-room.

If Captain Target had been moderate in his approbation before, the prefent fcene would have thrown him into ecftafies. Every thing was excellent; he eat voracioufly, met with all his favourite difhes, with wine peculiarly adapted to his tafte, and at the conclufion of his vifit he entreated Mr. Dudley to allow him the honour of confidering him in the light of an intimate. Mr. Alfop's bow urged the fame requeft, to which Mr. Dudley politely affented.

On

On their return home, Mr. Alfop, who had pondered upon the events of the day, without being able to fhape the chaos of his own mind into any determined form, refolved to found his friend's *real* opinion, that they might at leaft have the happinefs of agreeing in the fame ftory. A prudent fcheme, and the more neceffary, as the abfence or prefence of the applauded perfons frequently produced a wide difference in the Captain's fentiments. Finding him however fincere upon the prefent occafion, he commenced a warm admirer of the family at Stannadine, and heroically refolving to defend the caufe of injured merit, called upon Mifs Cardamum the next morning with the exprefs defign of telling her that he really thought Mr. Dudley a very good fort of man, and his daughter a pretty agreeable young lady ; adding as a clencher, that Captain Target faid fo too.

Whoever confiders how rude it is to difpute any opinion which a lady has advanced,

or

or how highly affronting it is to commend
the features of another in the prefence of a
fifter belle, may form a faint idea of Mifs
Cardamum's refentment, heightened by the
painful fentiments which love and jealoufy
excited. She darted on Mr. Alfop a look of
fiery indignation, which on recollection fhe
turned into the fmile of farcaftical contempt,
complimenting him upon his *fuperior* fhare
of difcernment. Then turning to fome ladies who were prefent, fhe expatiated upon
the merits of young Mr. Inkle the new dra-
per, declared he was not only well bred, but
handfome, and fo refpectfully civil in his de-
portment, that fhe fhould not at all wonder
at his marrying a woman of fuperior education and large fortune. Amongft Mr. In-.
cle's merits, his never contradicting any body was pointed out with fuch marked encomiums, that poor Mr. Alfop, though not
very acute in his feelings, could not but obferve how highly he had offended; and feeling his courage unequal to the tafk of endeavouring

vouring to mitigate her refentment, confu-
fedly withdrew. As he was not at the card
affembly that evening, I prefume he fpent
it alone in all the agonies of diftrefs.

Happily our fex is of too gentle a nature
to fuffer our refentments to be as lafting as
they are violent. Mifs Cardamum met both
gentlemen in her walk next morning, and
courtefied with her ufual affability : nay,
her kind confideration led her ftill further,
for anxious to prevent any ill confequences
arifing from her late encomium on Mr. In-
cle, fhe took care to tell her companion
Mifs Dorothea Medium, loud enough for
the gentlemen to hear, that though the man
was very well in his fhop, and behaved civil
to his cuftomers, it would be very wrong to
treat him in the fame manner as one would
genteel people; for tradesfolks were very
apt to give themfelves airs, if genteel people took notice of them.

CHAP. IV.

Containing what may be termed a literary curiofity, being an extract from the journal of an old maid.

BEFORE the character of the elder part of the Dudley family could be decided upon in a fatisfactory manner, a new ftar arofe in the horizon. I almoft doubt whether the firft appearance of Helen at the Court of Priam excited more wonder and furprife amongft the Trojan ladies, than did the lovely Marianne Dudley, when in the full blaze of natural charms, aided by all the graceful appendages which tafteful art could beftow,—fhe burft upon us at our monthly affembly in full fplendor. So inconteftable was *her* claim to the praife of beauty, that even the invidious were hurried into applaufe. Mifs Cardamum was the firft who recovered from the general confternation. She ventured to obferve that though her features were very regular, fhe thought they

were

were rather deficient in expreffion. Mrs. Medium purfued the hint, and lamented the want of a certain dignity of manner and look, of which Lady Seraphina was immenfely fond, adding, " Now there's my Dorothea, though a plain girl, (hold up your head my dear,) fhe has more of that turn of countenance which her poor dear Ladyfhip fo much admired."

The incertitude of publick opinion has been exemplified by hiftories of degraded heroes and perfecuted patriots. I choofe to illuftrate it by an inftance from common life. As it was very natural for inquiry to be bufy about an objeft that fo ftrongly arrefted attention, we foon difcovered Marianne's independent fortune. Rumour on this occafion afted in her ufual way, increafing it at leaft to one hundred thoufand pounds; for the many-tongued goddefs always enlarges the poffeffions of the wealthy, in the fame proportion as fhe diminifhes the refources of the unfortunate.

We

We were likewife told that Mr. Dudley and Louifa were almoft dependent upon Marianne, who, like moft favourites of fortune, was capricious, vain, and haughty; and returned their kind folicitude to pleafe with whimfical indifference. No fooner did we know that the former objects of our diflike were lefs happy than we fuppofed, than all their good qualities burft in a flood upon us, and we alternately pitied and admired the modeft, the fenfible, and affable Louifa.

Thefe tender fentiments were confirmed by frefh news from Stannadine. John the errand-man had told Betty at the Poft Office, that a fine gentleman was expected as a fuitor to the younger Mifs. Every lady in Danbury was now out of patience that fuch a little chitty face fhould be preferred to her elder fifter: it furnifhed feveral pathetic differtations on the bad tafte and mercenary temper of men, and brought back to the remembrance of our fociety the golden days of youth, when female merit, unlefs obftinately

bent

bent on a fingle ftate, was fure of procuring
the regard of the other fex. Mrs. Eleanor
Singleton and myfelf enlarged upon the difficulty we had to avoid being actually wor-
ried into matrimony, in fpite of our avowed
declarations to the contrary.

I have often lamented the fituation of
many good ladies, who like myfelf may be
faid almoft to fubfift upon news, and are often forced to devour very unwholefome ali-
ment. The events which *really* happen in
a fmall neighbourhood, are not fufficient to
furnifh the fupplies converfation eternally
requires, without the aid of fiction. I have
often, though encumbered with my umbrella
and pattens, carried a piece of intelligence
round the town in the morning, which in the
evening I was forced to ftep out and contra-
dict. An extract from my weekly journal
will prove this obfervation.

MONDAY.

Mr. Pelham is come to Stannadine—
They will foon be married, for the mantua-

maker went over this morning, doubtlefs to receive orders about wedding-clothes. Memorandum. Mifs Cardamum fays they will have the clothes from a London warehoufe, and that the groom went to town yefterday about them.

TUESDAY.

Not quite certain which of the ladies Mr. Pelham addreffes. He was feen walking this morning with Mifs Dudley.

WEDNESDAY.

Mifs Marianne has pofitively refufed him —She may be a long time before fhe has another offer.

THURSDAY.

It is very odd, if he is refufed, that he ftill ftays at Stannadine. Perhaps he intends to offer himfelf to Louifa.

FRIDAY.

We have all been miftaken. The Houfekeeper told my butcher when he went there for orders, that Mr. Pelham is not come as a lover, but only as an old friend of the family.

Finally,

Finally, after Mr. Pelham's perſon and character had run through all the changes of handſome and ugly, young and old, rich and poor, amiable and diſagreeable, we ſent him back to his own habitation on Saturday. Now, though we could not diſcover the myſtery, there really was ſomething in Mr. Pelham's viſit.

Ever ſince Marianne's arrival at her father's, Miſs Dudley perceived an unuſual gravity in her air and manner; and with true ſiſterly affection as well as delicacy, endeavoured to encourage her to reveal the cauſe by a ſoothing tenderneſs of behaviour, rather than by a prying curioſity, which indeed never deſerves, and ſeldom poſſeſſes confidence. The timid Marianne at length ventured to unboſom herſelf to her ſiſter, by owning that during her viſit at Lady Milton's, ſhe had received declarations of love from Mr. Pelham, her Ladyſhip's nephew, a gentleman of handſome fortune and unblemiſhed character.

Louifa congrattulated her upon fo refpectable a conqueft, and expreffed the tranfport
fhe would feel at feeing her placed under the
proteftion of a worthy hufband; but added,
that probably fhe was not yet able to judge,
whether Mr. Pelham really poffeffed the re-
quifites that were effential to her ideas of
happinefs.

Marianne's uncertainty upon this fubject
did not arife from any doubt fhe entertained
refpecting the gentlemen's merits, or the poffibility of her approving him. She was fearful left Mifs Milton's affeftions fhould have
been engaged by her coufin, in which cafe
fhe would die a thoufand deaths before fhe
would be the caufe of blafting the tender
bloffom of her Eliza's latent love. She had
not indeed any grounds for this fufpicion,
but the friendfhip which fubfifted between
the ladies was of a romantick kind, and confequently was too refined in its hopes and
fears to be adapted to ordinary capacities.

Louifa was not cafuift enough to determine

mine the intricate queftion, whether Marianne ought to reject Mr. Pelham, on the poffibility that Mifs Milton might be in love with him. Knowing no other rules of action than the plain laws of equity and honour, how could fhe decide on a point, which I may fay was finely obfcured by furrounding difficulties? Had fhe pleaded for Mr. Pelham, Marianne had a variety of inftances of high heroick virtue to produce, not drawn indeed from actual obfervations of life, but from her favourite ftudies. She had long been an attentive reader of memoirs and adventures, and had tranfplanted into her gentle bofom all the foft feelings and highly refined fenfibilities of the refpective heroines.

After feveral days of cruel perplexity, in which fhe at length refolved to facrifice love (for fhe doubted not her own regard for Mr. Pelham) upon the altar of friendfhip; a fervant arrived with a packet from Lady Milton. The firft letter addreffed to Mr. Dudley I fhall tranfcribe.

'SIR,

'Sir,

' Though many years have intervened,
' fince your departure from England termi-
' nated an acquaintance from which I re-
' ceived the fincereft pleafure, I do not doubt
' your recognifing the writing of an old
' friend with joy. The warm efteem which
' your excellent wife expreffed for me and
' my late fifter Pelham, and the happy hours
' we paffed together in early life, induces
' me to urge my prefent requeft with an air
' of confidence. The many excellencies of
' your younger daughter have made a deep
' impreffion upon my nephew's heart; I flat-
' ter myfelf, Sir, that upon inquiry you will
' find both his morals and fortune unexcep-
' tionable. Should he be fo fortunate as to
' obtain the approbation of the young lady
' and yourfelf, I cannot exprefs the tranfport
' I fhall feel at receiving the child of my
' moft valued friend into my family. My
' daughter, who loves her Marianne with
' more than a fifter's fondnefs, is in raptures
' at

' at difcovering her coufin's attachment, and
' laments bitterly that a diforder in her eyes
' prevents her from addreffing her dear cor-
' refpondent upon the fubject. Mr. Pelham
' writes by the fame conveyance. Allow
' me, Sir, to hope that his propofals will be
' as agreeable to you, as the fweet object of
' his affections is to us, and that you will fix
' an early day for the vifit he requefts per-
' miffion to make. With refpectful compli-
' ments to yourfelf and Mifs Dudley, with
' whom I hope foon to renew a perfonal ac-
' quaintance, and kindeft love to my dear
' niece elect, (pardon the freedom of that
' expreffion,) I remain,

' Dear Sir,

' Yours affectionately,

' E. MILTON.'

CHAP. V.

*Female irresolution may proceed from too
much as well as from too little refinement.*

A MIND difpofed to enjoy all the.
agreeable circumftances this world affords,
would have confidered the letter with which.
I concluded my laft chapter as a pleafant
event, at leaft as an indifputable proof that
the Miltons actually defired the propofed alliance. But Marianne Dudley was too refined
to be thus eafily fatisfied. She doubted not
that her Ladyfhip ftated, as far as fhe knew,
the real caufe of Eliza's diftreffing filence,
but could delicacy, while labouring under
the pangs of hopelefs love, do otherwife
than endeavour to conceal its tortures, under
the affumed air of indifpofition? No, it was
too evident; Eliza was certainly in love.

Such were the reflexions which agitated
her bofom, when her father with a fmiling
air delivered the letter for her perufal. Lou-

ifa

ifa had informed him on his confulting her about their contents, that fhe believed her fifter was not indifferent to Mr. Pelham's merits; how then could he account for the ftrong diftrefs vifible in Marianne's countenance: fhe however, recollecting that her forrows were of too delicate a nature for her father to underftand, thought it right, if poffible, to keep them from his obfervation, and hurried out of the room juft in time to conceal a flood of tears.

Mr. Dudley returned to Louifa to explain this extraordinary circumftance, who perhaps thinking her fifter a little whimfical, difguifed her knowledge of the real caufe, and pleaded the perplexing terrors an ingenuous and reflecting mind muft feel at the idea of intrufting its happinefs to a ftranger's care. She took an opportunity of following Marianne to her dreffing-room as foon as fhe could, and found her juft recovering from a profound reverie. A happy and heroical thought had occurred. By receiving Mr. Pelham's

addreffes

addreſſes ſhe would be enabled to judge of the ſtate of Miſs Milton's heart; and if by her pining deſpair her latent love was con- firmed, generous friendſhip might at any time renounce its own happineſs, and even at the altar reſign the expeſtant bridegroom, who, if unwilling to accept the ſubſtituted char- mer, would be *no* hero.

She communicated this plan to Louiſa, who, happy that a treaty ſo agreeable to her father might at any rate commence, informed him immediately of her ſiſter's acquieſcence. A letter of invitation was in conſequence diſpatched, and the happy lover ſoon ap- peared at Stannadine.

If an open, ingenuous countenance, manly ſenſe, and eaſy accommodating manners may allowably inſpire the beholders with a ſort of intuitive eſteem; Mr. Pelham, who poſſeſ- ſed all theſe advantages, had a claim to the warm affeſtion with which Mr. and Miſs Dudley received him. They felicitated each other on the agreeable proſpeſt which the

propoſed

propofed acquaintance offered; and forgetting that the tie of relationfhip was not yet confirmed, received him with all the kindnefs of a brother and fon. He brought Marianne a letter from Mifs Milton, dictated with fuch apparent eafe and heartfelt fatisfaction, that even her fertile imagination could fcarcely ftart any frefh doubts on that head.

Yet fhe was not happy. She now began to be apprehenfive that Mr. Pelham was not the kind of character with whom fhe could enjoy that perfect and uninterrupted felicity which fhe was certain the union of two kindred minds afforded. In the firft place, he feemed much more gay and lively than was confiftent with the painful fufpenfe in which courtfhip ought to keep the lover's heart. His manner was unembarraffed, which was wrong; he was comfortable in her abfence; her prefence indeed feemed to give him fatisfaction, but not of the tranfporting kind fhe expected. He maintained his own opinions in converfation, and though he treated

c 6　　　　　　her

her with refpect, yet not with deference. In his addreffes as a lover, he fell far fhort of that kneeling ecftatic tendernefs, that reftlefs folicitude, that profound veneration, in fhort, thofe thoufand namelefs refinements, which fome call abfurdities and fome delicacies, but by which men, who really love, afpire to gain the woman of their heart. Confequently might fhe not fear that his attachment was not of a kind to render their future lives a ftate of paradifiacal blifs?

If my readers fuppofe that the lady's faftidioufnefs arofe from vanity, arrogance, or fpleen, they miftake the character I mean to delineate. It was long ago obferved that the virtues lie between two oppofite vices; thus is all our attention awakened to keep the ftraight path of rectitude, as the leaft deviation leads us into one of the extremes. From over-ftrained humility, from gentlenefs which had increafed to timidity, and from fenfibility indulged till it became a weaknefs, from thefe caufes I fay, and from a wrong eftimate

mate of life, the errors and forrows of Marianne Dudley are to be derived.

In her character I wifh to exhibit the portrait of an amiable and ingenuous mind, folicitous to excel, and defirous to be happy, but deftitute of natural vigour or acquired ftability; forming to itfelf a romantick ftandard, to which nothing human ever attained; perplexed by imaginary difficulties; finking under fancied evils; deftroying its own peace by the very means which it takes to fecure it; and acting with a degree of folly beneath the common level, through its defire of afpiring above the ufual limits of female excellence.

Left an objection fhould be ftarted, that the exhibition of fuch a character may be of differvice to the general caufe of morality, I fhall urge my reafons for maintaining a contrary opinion. I have looked on life with deep attention, and forefee no evils likely to enfue from impreffing upon the minds of youth, as foon and as deeply as poffible, juft

notions

notions of the journey they are about to take, and juſt opinions of their fellow-travellers. I am perfuaded that the imaginary duties which the extreme of modern refinement prefcribes, are never practifed but at the expence of thofe folid virtues, whofe fuperior excellence has ſtood the teſt of ages. I conceive that the rules prefcribed to us as focial and accountable beings, are fully fufficient to exercife all our induſtry while in this tranfitory ftate. I wifh to afk the fair enthufiafts who indulge in all the extravagance of heroick generofity, romantick love, and exuberant friendfhip, whether they really fuppofe it poffible to improve upon the model which Chriſtianity (our beſt comfort in this world and fure guide to the next) prefents for our imitation. If not, I would tell them, that fimple but ineſtimable code prefents no puzzling queſtion to tear the divided heart by contrary duties. It fpeaks of life as a mutable fcene, and it admonifhes us to enjoy its bleffings with moderation,

and

and to endure its evils with patience. It tells us that man is as variable as the world he inhabits, that imperfections mingle with the virtues of the best; and by the fine idea of a state of warfare, urges us to constant circumspection and unwearied attention. From this mixture of good and evil it directs our pursuit after the former, by teaching us to *curb* our passions, and to *moderate* our desires; to expect with diffidence, enjoy with gratitude, and resign with submission. It commands us, conscious of our own failings, to be indulgent to the errors of others. Upon the basis of mutual wants, general imperfection, and universal kindred, it builds the fair structure of candour and benevolence.

And do these writers, whose works generally fall into the hands of the younger part of the softer sex, *indeed* suppose that they serve the interests of this divine institution, when they excite the dangerous excess of the passions, by representing the violence of love, grief, despair, and jealousy, not only

as

as amiable frailties, but as commendable
qualities? Ought fuicide ever to be introduced by a Chriſtian author, but as a brand
of infamy to mark charaćters peculiarly de-
teſtable? Should the love of a man to a
married woman ever be foftened into an innocent attachment, or defcribed as a tender
weaknefs which he *cannot* conquer, confequently rather as the error of nature and ne-
ceſſity, than of choice? Why is the young
mind led to form hopes which cannot be rea-
lized, and thus, by barbing the ſhafts of difappointment, to add to the already ample
ſtock of human calamities? In youth we
ſtart upon a race, in which the difficulties of
the way generally increafe as we draw nearer to the goal; and inſtead of ſtrengthening
the refolution, and bracing up the foul for
the conteſt, modern writers generally teach
us to ſhrink at the firſt ſhock of evil; to
melt in tender foftnefs at woes of our own
creating, and thus to turn with difguſt from
life before the fun of our exiſtence has advanced to its meridian. Thefe

These romantick notions indeed generally leave us on our journey; but what is the confequence? Repeated difappointments four the temper, we grow querulous complainers, difagreeable to others and burthenfome to ourfelves; and at laft, not unfrequently do we arraign the wifdom of Providence for not having rendered this world a perfect, inftead of a probationary ftate; for not having given us the felicity it never promifed, or for having implanted in us defires which we ought to fubdue, fince our Creator meant them rather as trials of fortitude than as fources of gratification.

CHAP. VI.

The Author endeavours to get rid of the ferious humour which contaminated the laft chapter.

To thofe who have had the courage to follow me through the ferious conclufion of the laft chapter, no apologies for its contents

tents will I hope be neceſſary; and I am certain all my well-bred readers will exerciſe their uſual privilege of ſkipping over the un-intereſting page. For their ſakes, therefore, I ſhall immediately reſume the narrative, pre-miſing, to conciliate their regard, that though I live in retirement, I know too much of the manners of the world, ever to expeᏟ even momentary attention to a moral reproof, when it attacks a reigning foible. And indeed, ſince youth and affluence ge-nerally proteᏟ their poſſeſſors from many re-al calamities, and as a certain portion of for-row ſeems neceſſary in the compoſition of human affairs; it would perhaps be cruel to perſuade the gay world to forget the many *pretty little* ſubjeᏟs of complaint, and all the agreeable viciſſitudes which the fairy re-gions of *imaginary* diſtreſs amply ſupply.

In returning to my hiſtory I ſhall illuſtrate this poſition. Can the calm ſatisfaᏟion a young woman, who thinks and acts in a common way, would receive from the

the addreffes of fuch a lover as Mr. Pelham,
be half fo enchanting as the fweet perturba-
tions, the delightful emotions, which a fuperior turn of fentiment excited in Marianne's
breaſt ?   Now elevated by the hope that he
would refine into an Orondates, now agonized by the idea that he had nothing of
true fenfibility in his compofition. From
her early childhood ſhe had maintained a voluminous correfpondence with Mifs Milton;
but on the prefent occafion ſhe was deprived
of all the confolation which pouring out her
foul to her Eliza would have afforded, by
that young lady's warm efteem for her coufin.   Mifs Dudley's fincere affection and ac-
knowledged prudence pointed her out as a
proper confidante, but unfortunately ſhe
wanted the grand requifite, for Louifa had
fo little fentiment, that ſhe was more inclined to laugh at her fifter's apprehenfions,
than to pour balm into the wound. Marianne
was therefore compelled to confine her
forrows almoſt wholly to her own bofom.

O3

On the contrary, Mr. Pelham was fo thoroughly fatisfied with his reception that he impatiently wifhed for an alliance with a family truly eftimable in all its branches. The romantick turn of his fair miftrefs did not indeed efcape his penetration, and he once dared to rally her upon the fubject; but perceiving it only increafed the ferioufnefs of her features, he carefully avoided again introducing it. He had delicacy enough to be tender of the failings of the woman whom he loved, and enough of love to be convinced, that the fweetnefs of her temper and the goodnefs of her heart would conquer the little errors which a romantick propenfity had engrafted upon her inexperienced mind; at leaft would prevent them from ever giving pain to an affectionate hufband. He hoped a little commerce with the world, to which fhe was almoft a ftranger, would divert her thoughts from their prefent train, and he anticipated the agreeable profpect of her laughing in a few years at her former enthufiafm.

Soon

Soon after he left Stannadine he was invited to Milton-Hall, to join in the festivities which were intended to welcome the return of her Ladyship's only son from the Indies; where he had refided feveral years in a military ftation, and amaffed a fortune fufficient to reftore that ancient family to the refpeftability it formerly poffeffed. At this happy meeting, Mr. Pelham's agreeable profpefts were difcuffed amongft other family topicks. He fpoke of the merits of Mr. and Mifs Dudley in fuch warm terms of recommendation, that Sir William Milton's impatience to be introduced to thefe eftimable charafters, could not confine its defire of gratification till after his coufin's nuptials. The privileges allowed to an accepted lover, feemed to juftify a requeft to accompany him on his next vifit to the Dudleys, and Mr. Pelham, not a little proud of his Marianne's attraftions, had no objeftion to introduce her to his friend.

Nature

Nature indeed had been far lefs liberal to
Sir William than to the other gentleman.
To judge by his countenance, a gloomy fufpicious foul feemed to lour from under his
dark bent eye-brows, and the air of confcious hauteur, which accompanied all his actions, rendered even his condefcenfions
painful and mortifying. He had been too
long accuftomed to the fervile adulation of
the eaft, to recollect that freeborn Britons
are feldom inclined to admit the claims of
wealth and arrogance, if men poffefs no fuperior title to refpect and efteem. So ftriking was his appearance, that even the candid
Louifa told her fifter, that, if Mr. Pelham's
countenance had been as unpleafing, fhe
would have confidered her apprehenfions of
future unhappinefs to have been rational.

But though Mifs Dudley drew thefe un-
favourable conclufions from Sir William's manner, he faw in her's an enchanting grace which enforced his approbation. Never did eafy fweetnefs of temper,
modeft fenfe, polifhed affability, and ftrict
                                   propriety

propriety of expreffion and behaviour, appear
more amiable than in the worthy Louifa.
Thefe were the qualities which he moft defired in a companion for life, and conceiving
the propofals he had it in his power to make
too ample to admit of hefitation, he foon requefted a private conference with Mr. Dud-
ey, and afked his permiffion to addrefs his
elder daughter.

The fond father would have rejoiced, if
the man who afpired to the juftly efteemed
darling of his heart had been more apparently amiable. He anfwered with hefitation.
His daughter's choice was free, and he fhould
limit his interference to the character of an
advifer; but he added, the liberality of Sir
William's propofals required at leaft frank-
nefs on his part. It might be expected from
his ftyle of living, that Louifa's fortune would
prove adequate to the expectations Sir William Milton might juftly pretend to. It
was unhappily the reverfe. Indeed on declining the mercantile bufinefs, he imagined

he

he had fecured an handfome income, but the deftruction of that part of Barbadoes in which his eftate lay, together with the doubtful credit of a great mercantile houfe, in whofe concerns he had from motives of private friendfhip rafhly embarked all his perfonal property, rendered his daughter's fortune at beft but problematical; and he feared he could rate her value at little more than a mind, which would not be deftitute of comforts, even in depreffed circumftances.

Sir William was more gratified than difappointed at this difcovery. The idea of laying a wife under an obligation was rather flattering to his pride; and fince his fortune was too large to confine his views in plans of expenditure, he was defirous of marrying a woman who having no claim of her own to affluence, might enjoy the wealth to which he gave her a title, with exultation and gratitude. He told Mr. Dudley, that, thanks to fortune and his own exertions, he had no reafon to confider pecuniary conveniences. Mifs Dudley

Dudley was the woman he should prefer to all others, and he even wished her to bring him nothing more than her merit and her affections.

There was such an air of generosity in the above declaration, that Mr. Dudley condemned himself for having yielded to erroneous and uncharitable prepossessions. He promised to introduce him to his daughter, as an admirer whose pretensions met his approbation; and then retired to consider of the most likely means to render his mediation successful. He recollected that when they discussed the characters of their visitants the preceding evening, Louisa had spoken of Sir William in terms of such strong disapprobation, and drawn a parallel between him and Mr. Pelham so manifestly to Sir William's disadvantage, that Mr. Dudley thought proper gently to check her warmth, as rather indicative of the rashness of a precipitate conclusion, than of the dispassionate, candid judgment he wished her to form.

D She

She yielded with placid fubmiffion to his re-
proofs, and allowed the force of the extenuating circumftances he urged in Sir William's behalf; but, reflecting upon the circumftance, Mr. Dudley thought he perceived her acquiefcence had rather proceeded from deference than from conviction.

CHAP. VII.

Extremely dull.

MR. Dudley haftened to Louifa's
apartment, impatient to difcufs the important fubject which occupied his attention.
He intended to ftate with emphafis and pre-
cifion the reafons which induced him to ac-
cede to Sir William's offers, and to exert
his own influence over Louifa's mind to en-
fure their fuccefs; but ere he had proceeded
far, the young lady's apprehenfions took
the alarm. She funk upon her knees, and
clafping her father's hands, with eyes fwimming in tears, and looks full of anxiety and
confternation, exclaimed, My deareft Sir,
do

do not marry me to Sir William Milton."

To give pain to that bofom which had been the faithful repofitory of his fecrets and forrows; to afflict the dutiful and amiable child, to whofe love and fympathy he had ever fled as a refuge from injury, and a cure for difappointment; was more than Mr. Dudley's refolution could fupport. He tenderly raifed her, affured her of his unremitting tendernefs, and hurried out of the room to give vent to the expreffion of that concern his fwelling heart could fcarcely retain.

When alone, and removed from the influence of her powerful tears, he recollected that till fhe was in poffeffion of the whole argument, her decifion could not be juft. The fentiments refpecting filial confidence which fhe had always entertained, the known propriety of her conduct, and the calm command fhe had ever poffeffed over her affections, left him no room to fuppofe that her diflike to Sir William proceeded from the

ad-

addreſſes of a preferred, though unacknowledged lover. He at leaſt determined to
make another attempt, and fearing again to
expoſe his reſolution to the influence of her
ſoft diſtreſs, had recourſe to his pen, and
wrote the following letter:

‘ TO MISS DUDLEY.

‘ However lively my dear child's reluc-
‘ tance to read this addreſs may be, it can-
‘ not exceed what I feel, while by writing it
‘ I diſcharge a certain, though painful duty.
‘ Let a ſimilar inducement urge you, my
‘ Louiſa, to weigh my arguments with atten-
‘ tion. When you have done this, with all
‘ the temper and conſideration of which you
‘ are miſtreſs, I give you my word that
‘ your anſwer ſhall be deciſive. The ſub-
‘ ject in diſcuſſion ſhall never more be re-
‘ vived, if you perſiſt in your refuſal.

‘ Have I too highly rated your confi-
‘ dence in me, by ſuppoſing that you are ac-
‘ tually free from the impulſe of a prior at-
‘ tachment, and conſequently at liberty to

govern

' govern your heart by the dictates of your
' judgment? If, my love, from exuberant
' delicacy or extreme timidity, you have
' concealed from me a fecret of fuch impor-
' tance, this is the moment of difcovery.
' To urge you in favour of Sir William,
' while you feel a preference for another,
' would at once be cruel and unjuft. Fear
' no upbraidings from a father: my arms
' are open to embrace you, my heart con-
' firms your pardon, and my beft advice and
' affiftance are ready any way in which you
' fhall require their exertion; but till you
' affure me to the contrary, I will fuppofe
' you abfolutely difengaged.

' Did all men fee you with my partial eyes,
' I fhould have a propofal to announce, at
' leaft as unexceptionable as that which
' awaits the acceptance of your happy fifter.
' I do not fcruple to own that neither the
' perfon or manners of Sir William Milton
' are conciliating. His virtues appear to be
' of the ftern rather than of the amiable caft,

'and

‘ and I fhould conceive, that like our firft
‘ King Charles, he would foil the glofs of
‘ generofity by an ungracious method of be-
‘ ftowing favours. But when the heart is
‘ right, candour will excufe the reft. Were
‘ you lefs happy in the prudent gentlenefs of
‘ your own temper, I would not recommend
‘ an union with one who will probably claim
‘ indulgence. I depend upon the influence
‘ of your fweetnefs, to foften his afperity,
‘ or at leaft to enable you to fupport its ef-
‘ fects with patience and chearfulnefs. You
‘ have too much good fenfe to expect perfec-
‘ tion either in character or fituation, and
‘ though an accommodating temper is effen-
‘ tial to happinefs in moft marriages, I think
‘ my Louifa might be happy if her hufband
‘ poffeffed it but in an inferior degree.

　‘ I build my hopes on the juft fenfe he has
‘ of your merits. He generoufly fuppofes
‘ them an ample equivalent for all the ad-
‘ vantages wealth can beftow. How flatter-
‘ ing is this opinion to a doating father!

　　　　　　‘ How

' How fatisfactory, when he reflects that his
' darling child's virtues are of a caft that will
' bear the fcrutinizing eye of inquiry ! That
' they will realize the expectations of love,
' and elevate it into efteem! Am I too
' fanguine in fuppofing that a man, who can
' make the liberal offers he has done, will
' be influenced by the fweet and candid
' partner he has purchafed with his· liberty
' and his fortune ?

' You are, I know, above pecuniary mo-
' tives; on this head, however, I fhall in-
' troduce myfelf. Unwilling to difturb your
' peace, I have as much as poffible diminifh-
' ed my fears for the fecurity of the fleet, in
' which the little property I could preferve
' from the wreck of my fortunes in the Weft-
' Indies, is embarked. I have alfo wholly
' concealed my doubts, which are now al-
' moft certainties, refpecting the refponfibi-
' lity of the Meffieurs Tonnereaus. Sir
' William knows on what a doubtful contin-
' gence your fortune depends, and I never
' fhall

' fhall forget the air of pleafure his counte-
' nance affumed at the difcovery; as if he
' till then doubted the validity of his preten-
' fions to you. Confider, my child, if my
' apprehenfions are juft (and I affure you I
' did not lightly entertain them) how I am to
' fupport the thought that my rafh and fatal
' confidence has reduced you to penury.
' You will, I know, endure adverfity with
' dignity and patience, but every fmile in
' which you meekly drefs your countenance
' to receive me, will be a dagger in my con-
' fcious heart.

' To you, who have been bred in afflu-
' ence, the perplexities of a limited fortune
' are inconceivable while at a diftance; but
' when experienced they will be moft poig-
' nantly felt. I knew them, my child, in
' my early years. My excellent father pof-
' feffed every defirable bleffing except a com-
' petence. He was, you know, a Clergy-
' man, living upon fmall perferment. His
' numerous family was at once his delight and
' his

' his perplexity, the fource of all his plea-
' fures, and the object of all his fears. Even
' his firm philofophick mind and fteady con-
' fidence in Heaven, fometimes yielded to
' the diftreffes which the numerous wants of
' his children occafioned; and the fear of
' leaving his almoft adored wife, and his or-
' phans deftitute, to the mercy of the world,
' grew as his health declined almoft infup-
' portable.

 ' From fuch pangs, my Louifa, I would
' fecure you, by an union with a worthy,
' though perhaps not a highly amiable man.
' Perfonal confiderations are beneath your
' attention. Defect in character is the una-
' voidable lot of humanity. If you have dif-
' covered no reafons for difapprobation,
' ftronger than thofe you ftated laft night,
' and your heart is *totally* difengaged, I
' truft your affections may be taught by gra-
' titude to flow in the channel which judgment
' prefcribes. If your repugnance is ftill in-
' furmountable, do not add to your perplex-
' ity by the apprehenfion of my difpleafure.

' The

' The reasons which influenced my child are
' at least entitled to my respect. Whether
' I possess a cottage or a palace, my Louisa
' is most welcome to the comforts it affords.
' The companion of my prosperity shall teach
' me to support adversity: her happiness not
' her aggrandisement is the wish of her

' Most affectionate father,

' RICHARD DUDLEY.'

CHAP. VIII.

*An attempt at novelty. Louisa reluctantly
consents to admit the addresses of a rich
young baronet.*

MISS Dudley had scarcely recovered
from the involuntary shock, which the first
intimation of Sir William's Milton's attachment had occasioned, when her father's letter arrived. She had persuaded herself that
either entreaty or fortitude might prevent
the intended tie. The contents of the letter
would at least have convinced her, that some-
thing could be urged in justification of Mr.
Dudley's wishes; but the sentiments of love
and

and confidence with which it was replete, forcibly appealing to her heart, and calling
forth the mingled fentiments of filial piety
and ftrong reluctance, too much agitated
her mind to allow her to reafon. She fat a
few moments trembling and filent, and then
burft into tears.

Marianne, who at that moment entered
the dreffing-room, was fhocked at her fifter's
pale and agitated countenance. She flew towards her: "You are ill, my dear Louifa,
for Heaven's fake, fpeak." Mifs Dudley
faintly attempted to fmile. "My diforder,"
faid fhe, "is nothing but an apprehenfive
mind; you have a claim to my confidence.
Sir William Milton has made propofals refpecting me to my father, which I am griev-
ed to fay he approves."

"Ah, my love," exclaimed Marianne,
"how fimilar is our fate! I have endured
too much not to pity you; but what are your
refolves?" "If poffible, to comply with
my father's wifhes," returned Louifa. "Heroick girl! The refolution is worthy of

yourself. I have at laft brought my mind to the fame determination. Hearts like ours, my Louifa, can never know felicity but in the converfe of a kindred foul; yet though our future lives muft pafs in one fad joylefs tenour, it will be a fupport in our fuffer-ings, to reflect that we have complied with the paternal injunction. This thought will be a balm to all our woes, and will at laft render the bed of death eafy. I have long ago given up every hope, except what I derive from your affection. My fifter in blood and now alfo in affliction."

Louifa was too ferioufly difcompofed to anfwer this addrefs in any other way than by a tender preffure of her hand. She beg-ged to be alone. " I muft," faid fhe, " be prompt in my reply; as it will be decifive, I ought to deliberate." Marianne expreffed how deeply fhe felt for her, and with-drew.

Louifa now exerting all her natural forti-tude, again perufed her father's letter. " Shall I," faid fhe, " fhrink from a duty,

when

when encouraged by example as well as pre-
cept ?"

To her father's inquiry refpecting a pre-
engagement, fhe fancied fhe could give a
clear and fatisfactory negative. She had not
entirely efcaped the addreffes of lovers, but
neither their affiduities nor their offers ever
excited more than a momentary attention.
How then could fhe explain the violence of
her averfion to Sir William? and yet the
more fhe probed her heart, the more fenfible fhe was of her reluctance.

Her father's obfervation in the fucceeding
paragraph, refpecting the fuperior merit of
her happier fifter's lover, brought Mr. Pelham before her eyes, in all that ftrong light
of contraft in which her fancy had often exhibited him. Her imagination winged by
the wifh, that he, inftead of Sir William, had
been the lover Mr. Dudley propofed, did
not eafily return from its excurfive flight, to
recollect that wifhes are the weak refort of a
querulous, impaffioned mind. Her foul was
above

above envy, and though the brightnefs of
Marianne's profpects feemed to deepen the
gloom of her own, fhe perceived her fifter
was not in reality happier. By her, the real
excellencies of Mr. Pelham's conduct were
overlooked, while fhe continued in fanciful
purfuit after an imaginary undefined good.
Louifa again endeavoured to avoid the fault
fhe faw in her fifter, and to make the beft of
her own lot; but in endeavouring to think
of Sir William, the idea of Mr. Pelham again
returned. Her cheek glowed, and perhaps
for the firft time fhe had caufe to arraign the
rectitude of her heart. Deceived by the
native opennefs of her temper, fhe fuppofed
fhe was only cultivating the friendfhip a fifter ought to feel for a fifter's lover, when her
attention was rivetted to all Mr. Pelham's
words and actions. Without her own con-
currence, or indeed knowledge, her thoughts
during her hours of retirement had been
chiefly appropriated to him. Conviction
flafhed upon her foul, and fhe felt a momentary

mentary humiliation. I fay momentary, for no fooner did fhe difcover the 'ftate of her heart, than fhe determined that Sir William Milton fhould not owe his rejection to the preference fhe fecretly entertained for a gentleman, who would foon probably be her fifter's hufband. Marianne's whimfical irrefolution afforded her neither hope nor juftification; Mr. Pelham's attachment was avowed, and his miftrefs muft, if true to her own happinefs, reward it. At leaft honour, delicacy, fifterly love, all forbade her to indulge a paffion, which could only end in guilt or difappointment.

On returning to the letter, her father's fentiments confirmed her noble refolution. He praifed her prudence; ought fhe to difgrace his judgment?. He fpoke of her as his deareft confolation; and fhould fhe add to his griefs or embarraffments? What a tranfport to be able to fupport an unfortunate but almoft adored father! Could love, even innocent happy love, fupply a more exalted blifs?   Deter-

Determined, with all the laudable diffidence of an ingenuous mind, not to truſt her reſolution to the chance of an hour, ſhe reſolved to write to her father, and to inform him of the acquieſcence with his wiſhes. There are ſome ſecrets which ſcarcely admit of being diſcloſed even to ourſelves. Louiſa's was of this nature. Reſolved to eradicate an attachment it would have been criminal to avow, ſhe judged it unneceſſary to mention to her father the reaſon which moſt forcibly determined her; ſince virtue, diſcretion, and ſelf-command told her it would not long exiſt.

'TO MR. DUDLEY.

' Dear and Honoured Father,

' Have you from my earlieſt infancy to
' this moment ever given a ſtronger proof of
' your affeƈtion for me, than the letter I now
' hold to my throbbing heart? You bid me,
' Sir, be ſincere; I have bathed it with tears
' of veneration, gratitude, and reluƈtance.
' The laſt was the leaſt painful emotion.

' I acknow-

' I acknowledge no prior attachment, and
' I truft I fhall be able to beftow my heart
' where your wifhes point. At leaft, the
' gentleman whom your fuperior penetration
' is difpofed to favour, may be fure of ac-
' quiring my efteem. Be pleafed to inform
' Sir William Milton that I will endeavour
' to deferve his generous preference: our
' acquaintance has been fo recent that he will
' not expeft me to fay more. To you, my
' father, I will own that the unbounded afflu-
' ence he poffeffes has to me no other charm,
' than that it will enable me to relieve
' every anxious care which oppreffes your
' heart. You invite me to partake of your
' cottage. Oh, for a fanftuary fafe from
' every misfortune in which I might infhrino
' you!   LOUISA DUDLEY.'

The agitation of Mifs Dudley's mind was
too great to permit her to write with a fteady
hand. Mr. Dudley, upon receiving it, haftened to her apartment. " I have," faid he,
tenderly embracing her, " received a letter
which

which does honour to your filial piety and
virtue. The pleasure I received from it
would have been unmixed, could I have
forgotten that what gave transport to my
heart, was perhaps the source of bitter pangs
to yours."

"You have convinced my reason, Sir,"
replied Louisa; "and if I did not attempt
to act according to its rules, I should de-
serve contempt rather than pity. But does
Sir William know my answer? I trust he
does not press an immediate interview."

"I have avoided Sir William," said Mr.
Dudley, "and for the present shall. You
have rather told me what you wish to do, than
what you are able to perform. It is not ne-
cessary that he should be immediately accepted, but after he is, it is highly important
that he should not be able to tax your conduct with levity or caprice. Recollect yourself, my child: the subject in debate respects
your future happiness, yet it is not more important

portant to yourfelf than to me. If the pleas
I have urged give you pain, forget them."

"Your tendernefs," faid Louifa, melting
into tears, " is lefs pleafing, as it implies a
want of that confidence in my ftrength of
mind, which I wifh to infpire. Have I, Sir,
forfeited your efteem? I mean to be ingenuous; Sir William fhall know my errors
and defects. I will tell him at our firft interview, that, perhaps I can never return his
difinterefted regard with warm attachment;
but that he fhall poffefs my duty, efteem, and
gratitude. If this declaration fatisfies him, I
will be his."

" And fhall I prepare him, my love," faid
Mr. Dudley, " by telling him that at the apprehenfion of that interview you trembled,
turned pale, and eagerly caught hold of my
hand? My dear child, you never appeared
more deferving of my efteem than at this
moment. But be not precipitate; if your
refolution is well founded, it will be the
fame to-morrow morning. We fhall, you
know,

know, have company to dinner; refume your compofure, and judge of your lover's behaviour. Trivial circumftances fometimes prove a true index to the heart, and may his be worthy of yours!"

Mr. Dudley preffed his daughter's hand between his, and withdrew, rightly judging that fhe would be better enabled to tranquillize her mind by refleftion, than by a further difcuffion of the painful fubjeft.

CHAP. IX.

A converfation piece, concluded by a fong.

THE benignant fmile with which Mifs Dudley performed the honours of her father's table this day, was not the fatisfaftory glow of a delighted heart, but the placid fweetnefs of a dignified and benevolent mind. Politenefs and attention were fo habitual to her, that it was impoffible for any of the guefts to complain of negleft, though her bofom was throbbing with fenfations of the

moft

moft painful nature. Determined to give
the pleafures fhe could not feel, fhe fmothered her fighs with fuch care, that even Mr.
Dudley's watchful eye could not difcover
her ferenity to be only affumed; and he con-
gratulated himfelf that the alliance which
promifed to fupport his tottering fortunes,
would alfo confirm his Louifa's happinefs.

The next interefting figure in the groupe
was Mr. Pelham, but as he really was as
much at eafe as he appeared, his merit muft
rank below the mild cheerfulnefs of Mifs
Dudley. His lively fenfe and attentive
good humour, while it feemed only folicitous
to call forth the various talents of the company, enjoyed the reverberation of the pleafure which he excited. Every body went
away fatisfied, and perfuaded that, next themfelves, Mr. Pelham was the moft amiable and
beft-informed perfon of the party. Swift
obferves, " that the perfon whom all agree
to pronounce deferving of the fecond place,
deferves in reality the firft :" I fhall not con-
trovert this opinion. The

The fair Marianne was not so universally admired. After she had left her sister's dressing-room, to divert the sympathising pain she really felt, she had recourse to her studies. The novel selected for the morning was of the mournful cast, and after attending the heroine through four long volumes of sentimental misery, the ideas of soft distress were so familiarized to her mind, and so heightened by Louisa's sufferings and her own perplexities, that during the whole evening she appeared more like the weeping April than the smiling May.

Sir William Milton exhibited a different cast of character. On his entrance into the room, he cast an observing glance from under his bent brows, on the company, which, though it consisted of all the *genteel* people of Danbury, he considered to be utterly beneath his notice. Wrapping himself, therefore, in his own conscious importance, he sat silently enjoying the superiority he felt. At intervals he threw his eyes upon Louisa,

not

not to fee how much fhe furpaffed the ob-
jefts around her, but to wonder why fhe
would take pains to render herfelf agreeable
to *fuch* people.

I do not hold forth this conduct as prudent. Few people are fo ftupid as not to
perceive when they are defpifed, and fewer
yet have fufficient fervility to fubmit to contempt. Thofe who appear to do fo are
guided by interefted motives, and it would
lower the hauteur of arrogance to reflect,
that the inferiors on whom they exercife their
ill humour, expect to be repaid for their forbearance. Wealth and rank have many natural advantages; mankind only afks permiffion to applaud and to admire them. A
nod from his Grace, a bow from my Lord,
or a fmile from the Squire, are a fort of
checque drawn upon our own vanity, which
we punctually difcharge with a large quantity
of commendation. All my neighbours went
determined to like the Nabob; yet even
Captain Target, though he had refolved to

vifit

vifit him at Milton-hall, returned without
being in raptures. To own the truth, every
body was too much piqued, to confefs their
own peculiar difappointment, but very kindly pitied other people's; and the unamiable
defcription of Sir William's haughty referve
concluded with, " To be fure *I* fhould not
fay fo, for he was very civil to me, but quite
rude to Mr. and Mrs. fuch-a-one."

No fooner had the party broken up, than
Marianne began to pity Louifa; " I trembled for you, my love, the whole day," faid
fhe. " How embarraffing ! to be forced to
entertain ftrangers, while your heart was
torn with fuch cruel apprehenfions."

" I could have wifhed," replied Louifa,
fmiling, " that you had been a little better
able to affift me. I was concerned to fee
you fo out of fpirits."

" And did you obferve it ? O you are
juft fuch a kind attentive friend as my
dear Grandmamma was ! But fympathy,

the

the boaſt of women, has no place in the bo-
ſom of men. You muſt now acknowledge
that I am right. If Mr. Pelham loved me,
he never could have been ſo cheerful and
volatile while I was ſo depreſſed. Sir William's behaviour was ſtrikingly different; he
hung upon your looks with the air of a man,
who only lived in your preſence. His ſilence
too and dejected air were highly expreſſive
of the anxious unaccepted lover. Indeed,
Louiſa, you will rule every movement of
his ſoul."

"I had rather be leſs important to him, or
elſe diſcover ſomething more amiable in his
manners," returned Louiſa. "His fixed attention diſconcerted me, but perhaps time
may render him leſs alarming. However, as
you are become the panegyriſt of my admirer, let me ſpeak in favour of yours."

"Giddy inſenſible creature," replied Marianne.

"How," cried Louiſa, "can you call him
inſenſible, who took this morning, unknown

to any one, a walk of five miles to relieve a worthy family in diftrefs? He is cheerful and agreeably animated indeed, but did you ever fee his mirth offend the laws of decorum, politenefs, or humanity? With what refpect does he fpeak of ferious and facred fubjects? His behaviour to Mr. Medium to-day is in point. How generoufly did he refcue that diffident man from the frothy jefts of Captain Target? What confequence did he give him in the eye of every one prefent, by the attentions he himfelf paid? I truft I fhould not have been negligent, but it would have been impoffible for me to have overlooked the dignity of the clerical character, while fuch a Mentor was prefent. How delicately did he divert from Mifs Cardamum the common-place raillery upon old maids, at the inftant too that Mr. Alfop was preparing a laugh at the Captain's jokes? Every one was delighted to fee the man of wit look infinitely more ridiculous, than the poor perfecuted fpinfter."

" My

" My heart was not fufficiently at eafe to obferve them," anfwered Marianne, half fmiling. " But I am rejoiced to fee you could. It certainly is a good omen for Sir William."

" I do not doubt," returned Louifa, re-collecting herfelf, " but that I fhall foon be able to difcover many latent good qualities in *him*; and then my prefent reluctance to his addreffes will difappear."

" Not if you are like me," fighed Marianne, " Mine increafe every hour."

" Then, for Heaven's fake, why not im-mediately refufe Mr. Pelham?"

" Can you, who fet me fuch a pattern of heroifm, afk, or need I anfwer? Filial piety forbids."

" You certainly miftake my father," re-turned Louifa; " he leaves you abfolutely free: he does not even influence you by giving his opinion."

" And can you imagine me ignorant what that opinion is?" faid Marianne. " His

eyes

eyes have told it me, every commendation he utters convinces me of his wifhes, and to thofe wifhes I devote myfelf a facrifice. I might even afk you, why he fhould be fo folicitous to fee you married, and yet indifferent how I am difpofed of?"

Louifa, who recollefted that her father did not wifh to deprefs her fifter's mind, by difcovering the misfortunes which threatened him, knew not how to reply. Marianne, who mifconftrued her embarraffment, paffionately exclaimed, "Speak, your filence is more diftrafting than certainty. If there be any reafon, it muft be that I have lefs of his affeftions, and if fo, loft, undone Marianne!" "You yield to a caufelefs alarm," returned Louifa. "Do, my dear girl, endeavour to conquer thefe keen fenfibilities. Be affured you have a full fhare of my father's heart. Let me perfuade you to entruft to him all your troubles. His tendernefs will relieve, and his difcretion will direft you. He has all the delicacy you can

wifh

wifh for in a confident; he will encourage
you by his condefcenfion: and fupport you
by his firmnefs. When you have opened
your heart to him, you will no longer doubt
his lively affe&ion. Tell me, Marianne,
will you take courage? Shall I prepare him
for the interview?"

After a little hefitation Marianne confented, and retired to confider what her troubles
and forrows really were.

In the morning Mifs Dudley met her father in the library. Her fmiling afpe& induced him to tell her, that, encouraged by
the unconftrained eafe of her behaviour yefterday, he had acquainted Sir William Milton with her determination; which he was the
more folicitous to do, as he perceived the
young Baronet hurt at being kept in fuf-
pence. He concluded with faying, that the
favour of an immediate introdu&ion had
been requefted. Louifa had fufficient prefence of mind to avoid trembling, and again
catching hold of her father's arm, fhe walked

to the window, and in a few moments faid
fhe would retire to her dreffing-room after
breakfaft, and would then fee Sir William.

She now recollected her fifter's requeft,
and ftated, as well as fhe was able, the irrefolution and terror under which Marianne laboured. Mr. Dudley, who had long thought
his younger daughter one of the peculiar favourites of fortune, was aftonifhed to find
that fhe alfo was fuffering under the " penal-
ty of Adam." He readily promifed his affiftance, but had Louifa been in a livelier
humour, it is poffible they might have mu-
tually laughed at the peculiar nature of the
fair mourner's embarraffment.

I formerly gave a reafon why I avoided
dwelling upon love fcenes; and indeed that
which paffed between Mifs Dudley and Sir
William was not very well calculated to do
credit to the defcriber. The gentleman was
confequential, the lady was confufed. The
fwain, at the moment he declared his high
fenfe of his miftrefs's excellencies, took care

to

to place his own advantages in a ftriking
point of view ; and the nymph, when he took
leave, could not help wifhing that he might
appear to greater advantage at his next interview.

Confidering it wrong in her prefent fituation to indulge reflections to his difadvan-
tage, Mifs Dudley ftrove to banifh them,
by adopting the following ftanzas to her
harpfichord :

SONG.

I.

Th' Idalian boy with frolick mien,
And Cytherea, changeful Queen,
 To Hymen's fhrine advance ;
Hope beckons to her fairy band,
With thefe the Graces, hand in hand,
 Unite in feftal dance.

II.

Pleafure attunes her filver fhell,
Of ever during joys to tell,
 Which mutual love fupplies ;
And fanguine youth, enwreath'd with flowers,
Tranfported views the white-rob'd hours,
 That bright in vifion rife.

But

III.

But not for me the joyful train
Bids Pleafure found that raptur'd ftrain,
  For me no Graces play;
Th' Idalian boy bends not his bow,
Nor does the torch of Hymen glow
  On me with gladfome ray.

IV.

Be firm, my heart, the conflict dare,
A father's grief, a father's care,
  Thy wifh'd affent beguiles;
And, powerful Virtue! be thou nigh,
Chafe the fond dew-drop from my eye,
  And drefs my face in fmiles.

V.

Nor let me with defponding gloom
Confine my profpects to the tomb,
  Or pine with mortal care;
When confcience whifpers mental peace,
Shall not the war of paffion ceafe?
  To guilt belongs defpair.

CHAP. X.

*Humbly dedicated to the improvement of all
fair Quixotes in heroifm.*

LEST the affection of my readers
fhould be wholly engroffed by the calm dignity

nity with which Louisa reconciled her mind
to whatever was unpleasant in her situation,
I shall dedicate this chapter to Marianne,
who was now immersed in a sea of troubles.

She so deeply pondered on the probable
consequences of the interview with her father,
that her mind was rendered too weak to derive any benefit from it. She alternately
threw herself upon the sopha, and reclined
upon the bosom of her confidential maid
Patty. She now feared she should never
support herself in the expected conversation,
and then again fortified her resolution with
hartshorn.

Mr. Dudley, at his first entrance into her
dressing-room, perceived his daughter's terrors, and endeavoured to divert them. He
praised the docility of a bull-finch, which, at
her bidding, chaunted the tune of " Ma
chere amie." He next commended the elegant fancy, with which she had decorated
Miss Milton's portrait, by connecting it to
her own by a broad blue ribband, on which

the

the words, "The bond of friendſhip," were
embroidered in ſilver foil. By thus leading
her attention from the ſubject, he enabled her
to recover herſelf; and in a little time ſhe
found courage to tell him, that ſhe wiſhed to
have his opinion whether it would be improper for her to diſmiſs Mr. Pelham.

Of that, Mr. Dudley anſwered, ſhe muſt
be the beſt judge, as ſhe knew what kind of
encouragement ſhe had given him.

"None, upon my word," ſhe replied,
"except permitting his viſits."

"The diſmiſſion of a lover who has received only that mark of attention," reſumed
Mr. Dudley, "is rather an embarraſſing affair; ſince it proves that the perſon you
thought worthy, when at a diſtance, is not ſo
eligible upon a nearer view. Will you, my
dear, ſtate your objections to Mr. Pelham?"

Marianne began her cuſtomary complaints.
"Their ſentiments did not coincide, their
taſtes were materially different, there was no
ſimilitude of ſoul, nothing to form that ſtrong
tie of ſympathy which you know," ſaid ſhe,
"muſt

" muft exift, or elfe there can be no certain expectation of felicity."

" Perhaps, my love," replied Mr. Dudley, " you will alter your opinion when you have heard what I am going to tell you. I have not entirely depended upon Mr. Pelham's very prepoffeffing countenance, nor the amiable urbanity of his manners, in forming a favourable opinion of his intrinfick worth. I have taken the liberty Lady Milton propofed, and have made repeated inquiries refpecting his character. The refult is highly fatisfactory. I am told that his morals are unexceptionable, and that his reputation for probity and goodnefs ftands very high. He is refpectfully treated by his fuperiors; a proof that he is free from the contemptible meannefs of fawning fervility. His equals efteem him, and he is idolized by his dependents; I fhould therefore think his benevolence and agreeable temper unqueftionable. In fine, I am told that he is a kind mafter, an indulgent landlord, an obliging neighbour, and a fteady active friend."

" Yet,

" Yet, Sir," faid Marianne, " you are only defcribing what I fhould call a good fort of perfon. Thefe are merely *common* virtues. How deteftable would he be if deftitute of them."

" Take care, Marianne, how you treat a good fort of man, as you term him, with contempt, or defpife the perfon who confcientioufly performs the ordinary duties of life. Providence has afcertained their value by their hourly recurrence. A man's family is the theatre wherein he can exercife every laudable quality. If he fail to practife them daily at home, he will never perform them gracefully before the eye of the world. Believe me, my child, the *common* virtues, as you ftile them, are the moft effential parts of the human character. They do not indeed dazzle our fenfes; but they gladden our hearts by a mild uniform luftre. To your queftion, what Mr. Pelham would be, if deftitute of them, I will anfwer, what many men are, who impofe upon the world as the poffeffors of fuperior merit;

merit; and who peculiarly attract the attention of the fuperficial part of your fex."

" Do not fpeak with feverity, my dear Sir," faid Marianne, her eyes fwimming with tears. " Your voice and look intimidate me."

" My voice and look then belie my heart," rejoined her father, " which at this moment overflows in tendernefs for you. Proceed, my love; have you any thing elfe to ftate?"

" Many things, my deareft father. Yet turn afide your face. Spare my blufhes. He is not, indeed he is not, the tender, refpectful, fympathizing lover, which my heart tells me is neceffary for my future repofe. He does not love me, at leaft not with that ardent affection, that deference, that affiduous timidity--But you fmile, Sir."

" I did, my dear, to fee by what a falfe romantick ftandard you eftimate your lover's worth. Have you obferved fo little of real life as not to perceive, that the kind of addrefs you talk of, is chiefly practifed by the defigning part of mankind, upon the woman whofe

whofe perfon or fortune is the objeƈ of their
defire? You muft know that marriage di-
vefts you of all this affumed confequence.
Law and cuftom leave the hufband mafter of
his own aƈions, and in a certain degree ar-
biter of his wife's. Whether your lover was
a fentimental fniveller, or an artful defigner,
the mock majefty with which you were in-
vefted could not continue in the married
ftate. The romantick part of love quickly
evaporates, and the fooneft with him who
has been the moft vifionary in his expeƈa-
tions. Think yourfelf happy if the kneeling
flave does not change into the Tyrant, and
compel you, in your turn, to endure without complaint, the whimfical indifference of
caprice, or the fudden burft of petulance.
Do not let my long leƈure tire you; but I
muft obferve that Mr. Pelham's charaƈer as
a man, is of much greater confequence to
your future peace, than his behaviour as a
lover. The latter diftinƈion will foon be
laid afide, on the former you muft depend
through

through life; and he who practises the other
relative duties, will seldom act wrong in this
more intimate and interesting connexion."

" But, Sir," said Marianne, " even in your
circumscribed and limited idea of love, some
portion of it is neceffary. Three years ago
I paffed the fummer with Mr. Pelham at Lady Milton's; if I *really* made an impreffion
upon his heart, would he have concealed
his paffion till my Grand-mamma's death had
afcertained my fortune? I then thought he
appeared moft attentive to Mifs Milton."

" If you, Marianne, are ferious in this
objection, your age affords the beft anfwer.
The character of a girl at fixteen is not fufficiently determined, to allow a prudent man
to look forward to a permanent connexion.
Nature has been liberal to your perfon, and
I perceive you are fond of making impreffions at firft fight; yet would you not wifh
your lover to fay with Juba,

> " 'Tis not a fet of features, or complexion,
> " The tincture of the fkin, that I admire ;
> " The virtuous Marcia towers above her fex ?"   Till

Till you are certain that the difcovery of fimilar perfection in your character, has not
fecured to you Mr. Pelham's affection, I
fhould advife you not to think him mercenary. Befides, recollect he was then a minor,
confequently he could not with propriety
think of marriage; and an attempt to engage
you in the many inconveniencies of a long
entanglement, however confiftent with the
narrow views of felf-indulgence, has little of
the generofity infeparable from my idea of
true love."

Marianne afked, with fome degree of ea-
gernefs, whether true love could difcover
any faults in the object of its affections?

Mr. Dudley was of opinion that it could,
as well as true friendfhip, for as the object
of either of thofe paffions was a fallible being, it was a proof that we indulged them to
a blameable excefs, when they precluded us
from the exercife of reafon. "I recollect,"
continued he, "the circumftance to which
I dare

I dare fay you allude, and will only tell
you, that if you do not renounce your romantick notions before you have been a wife
a twelve-month, I fhall think very *highly*
indeed of your hufband's politenefs, or very
meanly of the fincerity of his attachment to
you."

"I fhall never be converted, Sir," replied Marianne with a faint fmile. "The
picture you have drawn of a married life,
has determined me never to enter into it.
My heart tells me that if my hufband were
to omit any of thofe thoufand delicate attentions, thofe pleafing affiduities that won me
to be his, defpair and death muft be the
confequence."

"If you fpeak ferioufly, my dear child,
I fhall advife you by all means to adhere to
your refolution. Your motives for reject-
ing what I think a moft eligible offer, prove
that you have cherifhed inftead of fupprefs-
ed thofe painful fenfibilities, to which your
fex

fex owes its fevereft miferies; are you, my
love, who tremble at a breeze, fit to encounter the ftorms of life? If you feel
yourfelf unable to fupport a cafual unkindnefs, in which perhaps the heart has no fhare,
or a cafual error from which the mind, on
recolkâion, revolted, endeavour to con-
traâ your fphere of aâion, and to make
yourfelf happy with fewer bleffings, as you
cannot encounter their attendant forrows.
Marriage, like all other fublunary connexions, mixes the bitter with the fweet. Mutual confidence and efteem compofe the latter, and mutual forbearance muft be exert-
ed to palliate the former. The fimilitude
of foul, of tafte, and of fentiment, which
you talk of, is not neceffary. The ftrong
tie of fympathy often cannot exift; and the
delicate attentions and pleafing affiduities of
the lover, fo rarely appear in the hufband,
that if thefe circumftances *ftill* feem effential
to your peace, do not commit your happinefs

nefs to the flender chance of finding a human phœnix, but confine your fenfibility to the calmer enjoyments of friendfhip. A miftake *there* will neither be fo irretrievable, nor fo excruciating."

Marianne only anfwered with a deep figh, and Mr. Dudley, after conjuring her to give the whole argument a fair difcuffion, withdrew.

CHAP. XI.

A fpecimen of an Abigail's eloquence. Marianne appears in various points of view.

IMMEDIATELY after Mr. Dudley was gone, Mrs. Patty entered the dreffing-room. From the circumftance of having attended her young lady from her infancy, fhe imagined herfelf intitled to give her opinion upon every occurrence, and by virtue of liftening had made herfelf miftrefs of fome part of the foregoing converfation. She was particularly fhocked at the cruel advice given againft matrimony; nor could fhe have

have endured greater consternation, had
her lady's last present been spoil'd at the dy-
er's, or had any one assured her that the but-
ler had sent a billet-doux to the housekeep-
er. Those, who consider how advantageous
a young lady's love affairs are to an Abigail,
the certainty of possessing all the old ward-
robe, when the fair bride puts on her nuptial paraphernalia, and the possibility of further presents; must have hearts of adamant,
if they do not excuse Mrs. Patty's passion,
and forgive her, though she should be a little illiberal to Mr. Dudley.

"Oh, Patty," exclaimed Marianne, "I
am not equal to the troubles I must undergo.
I am weary of life."

"A great deal too good for the people
you are *confarned* with, Madam," replied
Patty. "Oh no, I am a poor helpless,
weak, inconsistent, creature."

"But if I were you, Madam, I would not
be *so* long. Mr. Frank tells me as how his
master is quite resolved about it, and means

to

to put the queſtion this very time; and I
know *I* ſhould not *argufy* long. I never
knew no good come of *ſhilly ſhally* doings,
I'd have him at once."

" I never will," ſaid Marianne, " nor any
one elſe. I deteſt the ſex. My father has
inſpired me with an abhorrence of all men."

" Never did I hear of any thing ſo barbarous," cried the indignant Patty. " I am
ſure you never ſhould have ſeen him this
morning, if I had thought what he was going
to ſay. Juſt as if it was not natural· to be
married, and as if people then could not be
happy if they like. I am ſure it is their own
faults if they *arn't*. Hate all men, indeed!
why the poor young gentleman will go mad.
Pray, Ma'am, don't uſe ſuch ſad words any
more, for you frighten me to death. But I
know what our old gentleman would be at,
I can ſee as well as another."

Marianne, who ſat deeply muſing upon
what her father had urged, did not hear one
word of Patty's eloquence; but paſſionately
exclaimed,

exclaimed, " O my Grandmamma, if your
fatal partiality had never diftinguifhed your
unhappy child, I fhould have had no caufe
to doubt the fincerity of my lover's attachment. Fortune, thou idol of mercenary
fouls, I deteft thy pageant incumbrance !"

Mrs. Patty, who thought money a very
good thing, and was feldom withheld from
anfwering by not clearly comprehending
her lady's meaning, readily replied, " Why,
certainly, Ma'am, when people love one
another, there is no need for money to make
them happy, and to be fure, young Mr. Pelham is very rich, and you may not like to
keep much company. But then cannot you
live quite retired, and do a great deal of
good, and be *vaftly* generous to every body
about you."

" I repeat that I hate him, that I am determined againft him," exclaimed Marianne.

Patty, who thought it impoffible her miftrefs fhould, of her own accord, hate
fuch a good-humoured looking gentleman,
was out of all patience with Mr. Dudley;

to

to whom fhe fuppofed this determination was
owing, and refolved to relieve herfelf from
the burden of the fecret, which fhe had faith-
fully concealed *three* hours. " Shame upon
them," faid fhe, " for a parcel of crafty folks,
and Heaven forgive me for fpeaking rafh,
but I can tell why he does this. Why,
Ma'am, I did not mean you fhould know
any thing about it, and to be fure I promifed
Thomas not to fay a word, but it is very true
for all that. Your Papa has outrun the con-
ftable I find, and as fure as you are alive
wants you never to marry, that you may take
care of him, and *the* Mifs Louifa he is fo
fond of. Thomas told me this very morning that things were in a fad poor way. His
mafter gets no fleep, but is walking about his
room, or elfe writing, and looking over ac-
counts. And he found a bit of an old letter,
fo he is fure there will be a crafh foon. But
I know if I were you, I never would be
made a tool of, and all to pleafe a favourite
fifter."

As

As wife people often defeat their aims by too great caution, cunning alfo frequently overfhoots the mark by too much craft. Patty's fpeech, inftead of awakening the angry malevolent paffions in the bofom of her gentle miftrefs, as fhe defigned it fhould, infpired the kindeft forrow for her unfortunate father; mingled with a regret too tender to be called envy, that his preference for Louifa was fo vifible. Her heart was really excellent, and fhe refolved not meanly to fupplant, but heroically to emulate her fifter. Mifs Dudley's motive for encouraging Sir William was now apparent, and ftimulated by her example, Marianne formed the refolution of never marrying, while her father's circumftances continued perplexed, but to dedicate the fortune fhe had juft quarrelled with to his fupport.

The heart is never fo eafy as when fuftained by confcious rectitude, and though the romantick turn of this young lady's mind, taught her to overlook little duties, it impetuoufly urged her to perform

form high acts of virtue. To increase the
merit of the facrifice, fhe refolved to conceal the motive, and after feverely chiding
Patty for her impertinent invectives, (which
fhe, with the true adroitnefs of her profeffion, excufed by exuberant declarations
of regard for her deareft lady,) difpatched
her to beg a fecond interview with Mr.
Dudley.

She met him with a fmile, which beaming
through her tears, befpoke the triumph of
fortitude in a feeling heart, and told him,
fhe had weighed his arguments, and felt determined againft marriage.

Mr. Dudley begged her to form no refolutions which might reftrain her judgment
refpecting a future connection. A lover
might appear better adapted to her tafte; but
as Mr. Pelham had not fufficient influence
to induce her to change the fingle ftate, his
difmiffion became unavoidable.

Marianne told her father her motives
would ever hold in force: " You will,"

faid fhe, " be left without a companion
when Louifa marries Sir William. Allow
me to fill *her* place in your affe&ions, and
to dedicate my life to you."

"You will ever preferve your *own* place,"
faid Mr. Dudley, clafping her to his bofom,
" and I truft my beloved girls will only leave
me to fecure to themfelves more tender and
affe&ionate friends, whofe prote&ion will
continue when mine is terminated by the law
of nature. Time, my Marianne, will, I
hope, diminifh that dangerous fufceptibility
which wars againft your peace, and then, like
your fifter, you will increafe my happinefs,
by giving me a fon worthy of my tendereft
affe&ion, if deferving of you."

Marianne's tranfport was unbounded.
Filial piety taught her to glory in the praife
of fuch a father, while confcience increafed
her joy, by fuggefting the honeft pride of
having deferved it. The only tafk remaining, was to difmifs Mr. Pelham politely, and
Mr. Dudley relu&antly undertook the painful office. That

That gentleman's mind was indeed prepa-
red in fome degree for this mortification.
He perceived the little progrefs he had made
in his charmer's heart; and as his attachment
rather increafed than declined, he felt the fevereft concern. Defirous of fecuring a woman, interefting even in her eccentricities,
he would willingly have framed his addreffes
to her tafte ; but as it is very difficult for a
man of honour to adopt the character which
he defpifes, or to fpeak a language foreign
to his heart, his unfortunate attempts at fighing Strephon were fo remarkably unfuccefs-
ful, that they only gave the idea of an ironi-
cal caricature ; and convinced Marianne that
he rather defigned to ridicule than to flatter
her opinion. But, though equally unhappy
in his natural and affumed character, he ftill
kept lingering near her, fafcinated by the hope
which love fupplied, that time might work
fome change in his fortune. A hope which
the favourable regard of Mr. and Mifs Dudley certainly ftrengthened.

The

The regret he felt at being deserted by
this poor support, was too severe to be softened by the warm expressions of esteem with
which Mr. Dudley qualified his daughter's
refusal. He repeatedly inquired if her de-
terminations were positively fixed; if entrea-
ties might not prevail upon her at least to
postpone his rejection; at length recollecting
himself, and fortifying his mind by the proud
(or shall I say by the prudent) consideration
that marriage could promise little happiness,
unless founded on the basis of *mutual* regard,
he determined to submit to his fate. At taking leave of Stannadine he impressed every
one with grief for his departure, except the
person whose approbation he had been most
solicitous to obtain.

CHAP. XII.

*Extremely useful to the author, giving her
an opportunity of filling her book, con-
trasting her characters, and displaying
great critical acumen.*

THE mythological fable of the combat
between Hercules and Antœus, may allude
to the pertinacity with which the human mind
reverts to its first designs. When our plans
are thwarted and disconcerted, the moment
of apparent defeat is that in which we most
zealously form the project of a fresh attack.
My classical readers will thank me for this
allusion, if it be only applied to a waiting-maid.

In short, the redoubtable Patty, though
one offer of marriage was absolutely negati-
ved, was still resolved to defeat her master's
supposed design, of fortuning Miss Dudley
with her lady's property : and thinking numerous lovers must at least unsettle her intention of living in " blessed singleness," she

began

began to debate upon the ways and means of raifing her an army of admirers.

The world is ever fo generoufly inclined to refcue a rich beauty from the vile durance in which fhe is kept by an avaricious, tyrannical, or capricious father, that Patty had only to tell her poor miftrefs's hard fate, in order to fucceed. Even Danbury was not without fomewhat of the chivalrous fpirit, and two Knights-errant iffued forth to refcue the captive Damfel. I choofe to fpeak according to the *real* intentions of the parties, for oftenfibly it was only one Knight, and an attendant Efquire.

Captain Target encouraged Mr. Alfop to make propofals, promifing to fecond him with all the powers of his addrefs and eloquence; which, to fay truth, he meant to employ to his own advantage if occafion offered. Let thofe who cenfure this as a breach of friendfhip, confider the fafcination of youth, wealth, and beauty, and they will, at leaft, allow that the Captain did not act an *uncommon* part. As

As it was very material to the fuccefs of their projects, that Mr. Dudley fhould not be apprized of them, referve in his prefence became indifpenfibly neceffary; and Mr. Alfop depending upon his friend for explanation, was not fufficiently pointed in his devoirs to Marianne, to enable her to difcover whether the frequency of thefe gentlemen's vifits was owing to the attraction of her own charms, or the good arrangement of her father's table. There was fomething fo unique in them both, that without any fhare of coquetry it was allowable to indulge a laugh at their experice; and Louifa often diverted her mind from the gloom of her own profpects, by rallying her fifter upon her conqueft, not only of young meum and tuum, but alfo of the veteran fon of Mars. Except the amufement which they afforded the ladies, their prefence added little to the pleafures of Stannadine. To a man like Mr. Dudley, poffeffed of refources in his own

mind,

mind, what is commonly called a good neighbour is rather a formidable character; and
Sir William Milton, now almoft an inmate in
the family, never fpent an hour with our
Danbury beaux, without difcovering fome
new quality to excite contempt. Neither of
my friends were fkilful in making difcoveries
of the mortifying kind; Mr. Alfop knew no
other criterion by which to difcover diflike,
than the blunt expreffion of " Sir, I do not
want your company," and the Captain was
perfuaded that Mr. Dudley enjoyed his long
military details, and that his happy, eafy, un-
encumbered, attentive manner had quite
conquered the Baronet's referve; becaufe he
often condefcended to laugh at his jefts; but
Captain Target was not bleffed with the
cleareft penetration.

Converfation is a delicacy of that peculiar
nature, that to preferve all its agreeable pun-
gency, many uncommon ingredients are neceffary. Mr. Dudley often felt diftreffed
how to amufe his guefts, and one evening,

to

to prevent the rifing yawn, without having recourfe to the famenefs of cards, he propofed the perufal of a Legendary Tale, which had afforded him entertainment a few days before. Marianne feconded the motion, declaring herfelf an enthufiaftick admirer of poetry. Her echo Alfop repeated her words, with the addition that he loved it fo much, that he always ufed to read the pretty things in the papers to his papa and his aunt Peggy; and the Captain enjoyed tales and ftories to his heart. It was at firft propofed that Louifa fhould be orator, but fhe, with graceful diffidence, defired leave to propofe an abler fubftitute, and delivered the manufcript to Sir William, with a fmile which almoft divefted his countenance of its ufual aufterity.

As my narrative is not now at a very interefting period, I am inclined to hope my critical readers will allow me the Goffip's privilege of digreffion. I will promife them, that my poetical epifode fhall be as condu-

cive

cive to *forward* my main plot, as fecondary
chara&ers and flowery illuftrations are, in
the moft approved produ&ions of my cotem-
poraries. Befides the ufual advantage of
filling my volumes, thofe, who choofe to
fkip over adventitious matter, will at one
glance know where to begin again. The
moral may recommend it to the few, who
ftill love to fee nobility clad in the refpe&-
able robe of virtue; and eminent rank defcribed in unifon with dignified fentiments
and generous a&ions.

RODOLPHO, EARL of NORFOLK;

A

LEGENDARY TALE.

Wifdom and Fortune combating together,
If that the former do but what it can,
No chance can fhake it.

SH.KSPEARE.

PART I.

'TWAS at the hour when evening's pall
 Hangs lightly on the vale,
The fongfters of the grove were mute,
 Hufh'd was each ruder gale:

The weary fwain had fought the path
 Which toward the hamlet goes,
To take his hard-earn'd frugal meal,
 And fnatch his fhort repofe:

When by the tufted oaks that throw
 Long fhadows o'er the mead,
The brave ill-fated Edgar led
 His much o'er-wearied fteed.

Bruis'd was his buckler, deeply bruis'd
 The cuirafs on his breaft;
And many a hoftile blow had fall'n
 Upon his batter'd creft.

F 6

Affliction

Affliction o'er his graceful form
    A soft attraction threw,
As damask rofes feem more fweet
    When wafh'd by morning dew.

As fad he mus'd on pleafures paft:
    On croffes that annoy,
And every bitter ill that taints
    The cup of human joy;

Sudden a tumult in the wood
    His ftartled ear alarms,
The fhriek of terror and furprife,
    The clang of hoftile arms.

Nor did the generous Edgar doubt
    His fuccour to beftow,
His heart, tho' full of fharp diftrefs,
    Still felt another's woe.

Now, near the fpot, he view'd a fcene
    Which might the brave affright,
Six ruffians join'd in murderous league
    Againft one gallant Knight:

That Knight with inbred courage warm'd
    Full on th'affailants bore;
A faithful fervant at his feet
    Lay bath'd in mortal gore.

Refiftlefs

Refiftlefs as the lightning's flafh,
　　His faulchion Edgar drew;
Nor does the dreaded bolt of Heaven
　　Defcend with aim more true.

Two quickly fell; the ftranger Knight
　　Th' unhop'd-for fuccour bleft;
New vigour nerv'd his finewy arm,
　　And fortify'd his breaft.

Sharp was the conflict! dire the fcene!
　　But Heaven is virtue's guard;
By arduous conflict proves its worth
　　To juftify reward.

All lifelefs fell; the refcu'd Knight
　　Survey'd them on the ground;
And knew them well, an outlaw'd band
　　For defp'rate deeds renown'd.

And now he fnatch'd brave Edgar's hand
　　With frank and courteous mien;
" How dear," he cried, " I prize my life,
　　Hereafter fhall be feen.

No low-born peafant haft thou fav'd,
　　No bafe unthankful churl;
Rodolpho is my name, a Knight,
　　And now of Norfolk, Earl.

　　　　　　　　　　　But

But let us to my caftle hafte,
    In yonder vale it lies;
And lo, to fpeed our tardy fteps,
    Night's deeper fhades arife."

They left the wood-crown'd hills, and fwift
    The winding vale explor'd;
And here a train with lighted brands
    Came forth to meet their lord.

Their veftures of rich cloth of gold
    Shone glittering in the light,
And foon the caftle's fpacious walls
    Burft full on Edgar's fight.

The ample moat, the lofty fpires,
    Each work of Gothick art,
Proclaim'd at once the mafter's wealth,
    And fpoke his liberal heart.

Obfervant of his honour'd will,
    The fervants crowded round,
And Edgar faw the ftately board
    With tafteful viands crown'd.

Rodolpho took a golden bowl,
    Mantling with cordial wine,
And graceful to his gallant gueft
    Confign'd the draught divine.

Then

Then to his train, " Whilſt we with food
  Our waſted ſtrength reſtore,
Go, bid the minſtrel's ſweet-ton'd harp
  Some ſoothing ditty pour."

The bard obey'd; love's woes he ſang,
  And then that deſcant clear,
Whoſe theme, the wars of ancient days,
  Enchants the chieftain's ear.

But as the wat'ry halo veils
  The ſplendor of the moon,
So look'd Sir Edgar's tearful eyes,
  Pain'd at the martial tune.

Rodolpho ſtopp'd the thrilling ſong,
  Then thus his train addreſt,
" That yet I live to thank your care,
  Be this brave hero bleſt.

Had not his arm from robbers fell
  A ſure defence ſupply'd,
I now had lain a lifeleſs corſe
  By faithful Oſbert's ſide."

He ceas'd; and through the ſpacious hall
  The burſt of tranſport reign'd,
Which, plainer far than ſtudied ſpeech,
  Great Norfolk's worth explain'd.

On

On Edgar each the ardent eye
  Of grateful blefling threw;
It fpoke the feelings of their hearts,
  It fpoke their virtues too.

The tumult ceas'd: now all retir'd,
  Save Norfolk and his gueft;
Again the Earl grafp'd Edgar's hand,
  And tremulous addrefs'd:

" Fortune around my favour'd head
  Has all her gifts diffus'd,
Nor yet has Love, to blefs my life,
  Her fweeter hopes refus'd.

My father from the Norman fhore
  With Royal William came;
He fhar'd the dangers of his lord,
  He fhar'd alike his fame.

Proportion'd to his foldier's worth,
  The King rewards beftow'd;
And, fince my father's death, to me
  Hath Royal bounty flow'd.

His honour'd patronage I boaft,
  His confidence poffefs;
I ufe my pow'r to punifh wrong,
  To mitigate diftrefs.

Thou

Thou brave preferver of my life,
  Or let me call thee friend,
My tongue would fpeak my heart's warm wifh,
  But fears it may offend.

In ev'ry gefture, ev'ry look,
  Thy lofty foul I trace;
The dignity of confcious worth
  Informs thy meaning face.

Yet I have mark'd thy frequent fighs
  Which, tho' in part fupprefs'd,
Awake a fear that fortune's wrongs
  Have oft thy foul diftrefs'd.

Say then, in all the ample ftore,
  The power, the wealth I bear,
Is there a blefling thou wouldft deign,
  At my requeft, to fhare?

Nor fear to afk; Rodolpho's life
  Is not of value bafe;
Some ample boon, fome princely gift,
  Should its preferver grace."

He paus'd; o'er Edgar's glowing face
  A deep fuffufion pafs'd;
And now his eye was rais'd to Heaven,
  And now on Norfolk caft.

"Oh

" Oh foul of honour !" he exclaim'd,
  " Too high the chance you rate ;
Which haply led me to behold
  Thy late difaftrous ftate.

For he who had a moment paus'd,
  Yet feen th' unequal ftrife,
Muft have a heart as bafe as thofe
  Who fought thy facred life.

Great Earl ! as at thy feftal board
  Obfervant I have fate,
And feen thy menials with delight
  Thy honour'd mandate wait :

My foul hath mus'd on all the wrongs
  I unregarded met,
From thofe who, tho' they fhare thy rank,
  Its duties ftill forget.

If to a poor man's fimple tale
  Thou canft indeed attend,
And to a loft and friendlefs wretch.
  Thy favouring arm extend ;

Know then, that Edgar is my name,
  And tho' of humble birth,
I boaft a parentage renown'd
  For uncorrupted worth.

My

My father, whofe ingenuous mind
    Confefs'd fair glory's charms,
Infpir'd his dear and only fon
    With love of arts and arms.

Fair was the promife of my youth,
    Beyond my rank or years ;
In ftudious lore, in manly fports,
    I rofe above my peers.

Impaffion'd memory with delight
    Yet recollects the days,
When all was pleafure, all was hope,
    Encouragement, and praife.

Deftructive to this fcene of joy,
    Love wak'd its fatal flame ;
Rob'd in an angel's fmiling form
    The dear delufion came.

Thou fay'ft, Rodolpho, thou haft lov'd,
    Thou wilt not then difdain
To hear me, tho' from grief diffufe;
    My tale of woe explain :

A Saxon lord, whofe lofty tow'rs
    O'erlook'd the vale we plow'd,
To grace his daughter's natal day,
    Conven'd a feftal crowd.

The

The martial fports, the conqueror's prize,
  My fwelling heart inflam'd;
I went, and victor in the jouft,
  The promis'd honour claim'd.

I follow'd with exulting ftep
  The vaffals of the lord,
To where the miftrefs of the feaft
  Beftow'd the wifh'd reward.

High on a ruftick throne fhe fate,
  With woodland lilies crown'd,
Her fimple veft of virgin white
  A cord of filver bound.

O'er her fair neck, whofe fnowy hue
  Her garland did upbraid, -
Half falling from a filken net
  Her nut-brown treffes ftray'd.

She turn'd on me her radiant eyes,
  Bright as the ftar of love;
She fmil'd; fo fweetly breaks the morn
  In yon blue vault above.

But each fine feature to defcribe,
  Demands fuperiour art;
Suffice it, their remembrance lives,
  Deep graven in my heart.

In

In tones, harmonious as the fpheres,
 My wifh'd fuccefs fhe hail'd:
I fhould have anfwer'd, but at once
 The power of language fail'd.

Kneeling I took the proffer'd prize,
 In humble awe I gaz'd;
A courtly victor would have fpoke,
 A colder lover prais'd.

Blufhing fhe fought the feftal hall,
 There 'mid the virgin choir,
Obedient to her father's will,
 She chaunted to her lyre.

The hopes of virtue were her theme,
 Its perils, and its praife;
Her heavenly looks might fpeak herfelf,
 The fubject of her lays.

O bleft tranfcendently! fhe cry'd,
 And worthy to be bleft,
Are all who, through the maze of life,
 Keep virtue's pure beheft.

Hard is the tafk, but toil and pain
 Invigorates the mind,
Which, finking on the couch of floth,
 Feels all its pow'rs confin'd.

Heaven

Heaven ne'er meant that man with eafe
  His wifhes fhould obtain,
He muft from labour's ftrenuous grafp
  The palm of triumph gain.

Oh gen'rous youth! if e'er thy heart
  To glory dares afpire,
Let active merit's guiding ray
  Direct the great defire.

By virtue, to the happy few
  Who love her laws, is giv'n
Heartfelt tranquillity on earth,
  And happinefs in heav'n.

She ceas'd! the numbers on my foul
  New energy beftow'd ;
At once love wak'd its thrilling flame,
  And emulation glow'd.

I felt the buoyant gale of hope
  A rifing fervour breathe ;
Vaft was her worth, but fanguine love
  Can miracles achieve.

Arms feem'd the neareft path to fame;
  I rous'd my ruftick bands,
And refcu'd from an outlaw'd chief
  Her father's richeft lands.

I con-

I conquer'd, but with generous pride
  All retribution wav'd;
I only fought my charmer's fmile,
  And fcorn'd the lands I fav'd.

But foon her father's piercing ken
  My latent love defcry'd;
Still will the confcious eye difclofe
  Thofe truths the heart would hide.

Mufing on every favouring hope
  Her gentle fmile convey'd,
As penfively one day I fate
  Beneath a poplar's fhade,

Her father came; Dar'ft thou, he cry'd,
  Of ruftick birth, afpire
To gain a beauteous lady's love,
  Who calls a Baron fire?

Prefume not on the little fame
  Thy fword by chance hath won,
Far nobler deeds, far ampler praife,
  Muft grace my future fon.

But to difguife thy daring love,
  No mean denials feek;
E'en now it flafhes in thy eyes,
  And blufhes on thy cheek.

My

My vengeance, yes, my vengeance, boy,
   Can arrogance reftrain;
Dare not beyond to-morrow's fun
   Abide in my domain.

He ceas'd—I trembled; 'twas not fear,
   A glow of honeft fhame;
A painful confcioufnefs of worth,
   Which yet I fcorn'd to name.

My ready hand had grafp'd my fword,
   But love the purpofe ftay'd;
It was the father of my fair,
   I fheath'd the half drawn blade.

Yes, at thy bidding I will go,
   From England I will fly;
Thou haft infulted me; 'tis well
   I frame no fierce reply.

Hereafter thou perchance may'ft hear
   Of my fuccefs in arms;
My country's foes fhall know how well
   I prize thy daughter's charms.

I turn'd—the glow of injur'd pride
   Supprefs'd each mournful thought;
I flew not to my father's arms,
   But Robert's banners fought.

                          Exulting,

Exulting, on my arm the crofs
  Of Paleſtine I bound ;
Nor doubted quickly to return,
  With martial honours crown'd.

How well I fought, let envious ſpleen,
  Let calumny proclaim ;
My native courage caught from love
  Enthuſiaſtick flame.

By thoſe I reſcu'd, hated, ſcorn'd,—
  Ah ! ſpare the painful tale—
I ſaw the hopes of youth and love,
  Of truth and candour, fail.

Tir'd of a ſcene where low-born art
  Could merit's due command,
Haraſs'd with toil, with ſorrow worn,
  I ſought my native land.

Theſe bruiſed arms and Knighthood's rank,
  In ſix long ſummers won,
I bear; to ſooth a father's grief
  For his unhappy ſon.

Yet ſtill I feel the fear of love,
  But why that fear deplore ?
It is the inmate of a heart
  Where hope exiſts no more."

END OF PART I.

PART II.

" Bleft are thofe
" Whofe blood and judgment are fo well commingled
" That they are not a pipe for Fortune's fingers
" To found what ftop fhe pleafes. Give me a man
" That is not paffion's flave, and I will wear him
" In my heart's core, aye, in my heart of heart."

SHAKSPEARE.

To Edgar then Rodolpho fpoke ;
 " What infolence deny'd,
By gen'rous friendfhip's grateful hand ·
 Shall amply be fupply'd.

And if the charmer of thy foul
 Thy high defert can move,
Her haughty father fhall be forc'd
 To court thy flighted love.

Oh ! Edgar, I have heard thee tell
 The ftory of thy woes,
And felt that int'reft in thy fate
 Which fympathy beftows.

Scorning the fnares which for my rank
 Ambitious beauty threw ;
No artful fmile, no ftudied glance,
 My cold attention drew.

Anxious

Anxious from every bafe reproach
   My tow'ring fame to fhield,
In fcience I amufement fought,
   And honour in the field.

As foremoft in the royal chafe
   I urg'd my rapid fteed,
One day I met a lovely maid,
   Attir'd in forrow's weed.

Slow fhe approach'd ; when near, fhe rais'd
   Her long, diforder'd veil,
And fhow'd a face divinely fair,
   But through dejeftion pale.

Wilt thou, fhe cried, Oh gallant Knight !
   A Damfel's fears allay,
And fwiftly to my lord the King
   My anxious fteps convey ?

I have a tale of woe to tell,
   Would I could accefs find !
All-righteous Heav'n, who knows my grief'
   Will move the royal mind.

I would have footh'd the fair diftrefs'd,
   But converfe fhe delay'd :
I led her to the green wood tent,
   Where ftill the monarch ftaid.

There

There in that eloquence of phrafe
 Which forrow can beftow,
Proftrate at royal William's feet,
 She told her tale of woe.

Her father, injur'd by a lord,
 Rank'd in the royal train,
Had dar'd to utter his complaints
 In treafon's guilty ftrain.

With purpos'd infurrection charg'd,
 Imprifon'd and arraign'd;
He faw his ancient honours feiz'd,
 His fair demefnes diftrain'd.

And ftill th' inexorable law,
 By mercy unconfin'd,
Had, to attainder of eftate,
 Life's deadly forfeit join'd.

The weeping beauty did not fear,
 Tho' want prepar'd to feize
Her, whom luxurious grandeur rear'd
 On the foft lap of eafe.

She fear'd not fcorn, tho' fcorn with joy
 The bow of fatire ftrung,
To fpoil the fhrine where flattery late
 Its gilded off'rings hung.

Her

Her gentle frame contain'd a foul
  In filial duty brave;
A father's life was what fhe fought
  From fortune's wreck to fave.

Stern is our royal mafter's foul,
  The guardian of the law;
Decided by the harfh decree,
  No lenient grace he faw.

Thy forrow for thy father's crimes,
  He cry'd, fhall ne'er atone;
Unpunifh'd, fhall rebellion's voice
  Infult the facred throne?

Oh! Edgar, never can my eyes
  Forget the awful fcene;
The horror of the lady's look,
  Her wild diforder'd mien.

Then muft he die? fhe beat her breaft,
  She groan'd in deep defpair:
Then muft my father die? fhe fhriek'd,
  And rent her flowing hair.

Oh! fave *him*, William! take *my* life,
  Let juftice have its due!
You had a father, but, alas!
  Your fire you never knew.

Whilft

Whilft thus through all the echoing tent
   The ftream of horror rung;
At once compaffion, wonder, love,
   Within my bofom fprung.

If e'en the monarch's eye auftere
   With pity feem'd to melt,
Oh think how deep my fofter foul
   Its thrilling impulfe felt.

I rifk'd my hopes; but let me fpare
   To tell each various art,
By which, to mercy by degrees,
   I mov'd great William's heart.

The pardon gain'd, I flew with joy
   The mourner to confole,
And in her father's prifon met
   The miftrefs of my foul.

By time fubdu'd, her pious grief
   Seem'd fix'd, but yet refign'd;
And to defpair's pale hollow cheek
   The calm of patience join'd.

She knelt befide her contrite fire,
   For him to Heav'n fhe pray'd;
Can beauty ever look more fweet
   Than thus in tears array'd?

                     I gave

I gave the pardon—then my heart
  A painful blifs confefs'd;
When the rapt father's eager arms
  His fainting daughter prefs'd.

Recov'ring from her trance of joy,
  I faw her tranfport fpeak,
Irradiate her yet doubtful eye,
  And flufh her changing cheek.

Affur'd, confirm'd, with winning grace
  Around my knees fhe clung:
She bleft me, but her eyes by far
  Outfpake her fault'ring tongue.

Now paffion fwelling in my foul,
  A fudden impulfe mov'd;
I caught the charmer to my heart,
  And told her that I lov'd.

At once I claim'd her fire's affent,
  And told my rank and ftate;
Boafting what bleffings I defign'd
  Should worth like her's await.

Edgar! I know a lib'ral mind
  Will own a terror here,
Left gratitude on gen'rous hearts
  Should lay a tafk fevere.

G 4

I fhould

I ſhould have waited till her eyes
   A ſoft eſteem confeſs'd;
Ere e'en in private to her ear
   I had my love exprefs'd.

I err'd, my friend;—my penſive heart
   Does oft its error own
When ſtead of love's impaſſion'd voice
   I hear cold duty's tone.

To-morrow's ſun (but can I then
   Taſte fulneſs of content?)
She ſeals with me the nuptial oath,
   Oh may her heart aſſent!

E'en when I left her yeſternight,
   And fondly breath'd adieu,
And of the morrow talk'd, her cheek
   Aſſum'd a paler hue.

Cold ſhe withdrew her trembling hand,
   And as ſhe turn'd aſide,
I ſaw a tear, the tears of love
   Would ſhe attempt to hide?

If to her ſire I breathe a doubt,
   He talks of virgin ſhame?
Of timid diffidence, which checks
   Chaſte beauty's baſhful flame.

                        Still

Still as I liften to his words,
 Each fad fuggeftion flies,
And all my future hours of life
 In profpeƈt fweet arife.

O gallant Edgar! think me not
 The flave of jealous fear;
The doubt that hangs upon my heart
 Is caus'd by love fincere.

Might but to-morrow make her bleft,
 How welcome were the day!
But while in talk we wafte the hour,
 The night wears faft away.

My brave preferver; from thy breaft
 Difmifs this gloom of woe;
And with thy friend, on feftal mirth,
 One happy day beftow."

" Bleft be thy morrow," Edgar cry'd,
 " The firft of happy days!
But fhall my father fay his fon
 At bridal feaft delays?

Six annual funs have feen his cheek
 Bedew'd with conftant tears;
Nor fhall thofe forrows ccafe to flow,
 Till Edgar's felf appears,"

" Go

" Go then," Rodolpho rifing, cried,
   " If fuch thy kind defire,
Within my caftle reft to-night,
   To-morrow feek thy fire.

Yet when his fond impaffion'd arms
   Shall fuffer thee to ftray,
Refleft that Norfolk owes a debt
   He lives but to repay.

The parting warriors now again
   The hands of friendfhip join'd ;
And Edgar, guided by a page,
   Sought out the room affign'd.

They pafs'd through many a marble hall,
   And many a lofty dome,
With cedar lin'd, or richly grac'd
   By Antwerp's coftly loom.

The wifh'd apartment gain'd, the Knight
   Again admiring gaz'd ;
For here, the wall with portraits hung,
   The mimick pencil prais'd.

On one fine painting, full in fight,
   He caft a ftartled view ;
A woman's form ; his beating heart
   Confefs'd the likenefs true.

                 " Know'ft

" Know'ſt thou that lady ?" to the page
 Impetuouſly he cried;
" It is Albina," ſaid the youth,
 " My maſter's deſtin'd bride."

" Thy maſter's bride, Albina, ſay—
 The Baron Siward's heir!"
" The ſame, but ſcarce the painter's art
 Could ſketch the peerleſs fair."

The page retir'd—the Knight alone
 Stood motionleſs in thought:
His lov'd Albina! for whoſe ſake
 He Robert's banners ſought.

The hope that Norfolk's friendſhip rais'd,
 On her alone rely'd;
Albina! ſoul-diſtraƐting thought!
 Is Norfolk's deſtin'd bride.

Beneath a canopy of ſtate,
 Which grac'd the proud alcove,
In vain the downy couch invites
 The frantick ſlave of love.

Still gazing wild with folded arms,
 The portrait full in view,
He drives love's arrows in his heart,
 And barbs their ſhafts anew.

       Yet

Yet from Rodolpho's boding fear
  A dawn of hope may break,
The tear that pain'd the gen'rous Earl
  Might flow for Edgar's fake.

" Oh blafted be that impious hope!
  Shall I the villain prove,
And fteal from him I moft efteem,
  The idol of his love ?

No, from this moment every wifh
  Defpairing I forego ;
'Tis better to be curs'd myfelf,
  Than caufe Rodolpho's woe.

Albina, tho' I muft till death
  Thy lovely form adore,
Thy lovely form, thy angel face,
  Shall feaft thefe eyes no more.

The ftory of my haplefs love
  Shall ne'er thy ear offend,
Nor fondly wake the pitying figh
  That wrongs my gen'rous friend.

That dear remembrance once beftow'd,
  Thus from my arm I tear ;
Would I could tear her from my heart,
  But fhe is rooted there."

                          Now

Now from his arm the ſtring of pearl
    He eagerly unties;
The ſtring of pearl Albina gave,
    His youthful valour's prize.

" Go, bracelet, to Rodolpho's foul
    A love like mine convey;
But teach the genial flame to burn
    With more auſpicious ray.

Go, when he binds thee on his arm
    An equal joy impart,
As once I felt, when firſt the ſmile
    Of beauty touch'd my heart."

So paſs'd the tedious night, now faint
    Approaching morning gleams;
And e'en ſad Edgar's woe-worn breaſt
    Receives its gladd'ning beams.

One wiſh remain'd, it was to footh
    The anguiſh of his fire;
He haſtens to the caſtle gate,
    There meets Rodolpho's 'Squire.

To him the bracelet he conſigns,
    To bear it to his friend;
And with it fay, that Edgar's prayers
    Will ſtill the Earl attend.

                    But

But penfive vifions of the night
  Had wak'd th' ill-omen'd dread,
That frefh diftreffes ripen'd hung
  O'er Edgar's fated head.

" Howe'er fevere on me," he cries,
  " The blow of anguifh falls,
May peace and happy love fecure
  Thefe hofpitable walls."

Then, all his deareft hopes refign'd,
  Upon his horfe he fprung;
The courfer's hoofs re-echoing loud,
  Upon the champaign rung.

The Earl arofe; he fought his friend,
  Then at his abfence figh'd;
And penfive, on his arm the pledge
  Of parting kindnefs ty'd:

And now his bridal train he call'd,
  And vaulted on his fteed;
'Twas fnowy white, of faultlefs form,
  And fprung from gen'rous breed.

Exulting on Rodolpho's cheek
  Sate expeftation warm;
And dignity and manly eafe
  Seem'd blended in his form.

                              Rich

Rich was his vesture; o'er his horse
 Embroider'd trappings flow'd;
But worth disclaiming outward pomp
 The Earl conspicuous shew'd.

At Siward's castle now arriv'd, .
 The joyful Baron came
To meet the splendid cavalcade,
 And bless Rodolpho's name.

" Thou gen'rous friend, to whom I owe
 My fortune and my life,
Come, ever welcome!" he exclaim'd,
 " Behold thy destin'd wife."

Slow was the fair Albina's step,
 And pensive was her air; .
Her face was pallid as the veil
 Which held her beauteous hair.

Tho' deck'd in bridal robes of state,
 Yet still her looks express'd
The victim of unhallow'd rites,
 For mournful orgies dress'd.

" Receive, my child,". her father cried,
 " Thy virtues to reward,—
Receive from thy fond parent's hand
 This brave and worthy lord.

No

No longer let thy maiden fears
   A coy reſerve impart;
Avow the love that Heaven approves,
   And give him all thy heart."

Albina now her penſive eyes
   On brave Rodolpho threw;
And when they met his ardent gaze,
   They timidly withdrew.

He ſnatch'd her hand: " What! ſtill, my fair,
   This cold and diſtant fear?
Does my Albina doubt my love,
   Or why diſtreſs'd appear?

" Oh! reſt aſſur'd, thou deareſt truſt
   That Heaven on earth can give,
'Tis but to make my charmer bleſt
   That now I wiſh to live.

" But yeſternight, when robbers fell
   My evening walk aſſail'd,
Lifeleſs on earth the ſervant ſunk,
   Who to defend me fail'd:

" When from my tir'd o'erpower'd arm
   Its wonted vigour fled,
And death's eternal gloomy ſhade
   Seem'd falling on my head:
                 " Memory,

" Memory, amid the tumult wild,
  Thy lovely image drew;
And thy foft woes, in fancy feen,
  Reftor'd my ftrength anew.

" When refcu'd by a gallant knight
  Whom Heav'n to fave me fent,
Life feem'd a nobler gift, fince life
  Would now with thee be fpent.

" But wherefore fhould I blefs the hand
  That did the gift beftow, '
If from thy fix'd, thy cold difdain,
  I only anguifh know ?"

" Let not my lord," Albina faid,
  " Such painful doubts fuggeft,
Nor think his merit fails to move
  Albina's confcious breaft.

" Can fhe forget, when fcorn'd, refus'd,
  In vain fhe mercy crav'd,
When, at the moment of defpair,
  His gen'rous pity fav'd ?

" If then his kind, but partial eyes,
  Deems her a meet reward,
Duty fhall prompt her grateful heart,
  To blefs her honour'd Lord."

END OF PART II.

PART

PART III.

" I am not of that feather to fhake off
" My friend when he moft needs me. I do know him
" A gentleman, that well deferves a help,
" Which he fhall have."
                                        SHAKSPEARE.

Now, while th' attendant train carous'd,
　　And drain'd the feftal bowl,
While mufick's various pow'rs combin'd,
　　Entranc'd each joyful foul,

Rodolpho, whifpering to his love,
　　His Edgar's worth exprefs'd,
And fhew'd the bracelet he receiv'd
　　From his departing gueft.

Inftant her looks, her trembling frame,
　　Confefs'd a wild alarm ;
While her fix'd eyes, with frantick gaze,
　　Dwelt on her lover's arm.

Vain was each effort to conceal,
　　Surprize fo highly wrought ;
She fainted ; but Rodolpho's arms
　　The finking beauty caught.

　　　　　　　　　　　　　　　Their

Their lovely miftrefs to fupport,
　　Th' attendant handmaids flew ;
Reluctant from her opening eyes
　　The thoughtful Earl withdrew.

Cold o'er his foul each doubt confirm'd,
　　Its painful influence flung,
And heavy on his bended arm
　　His head recumbent hung.

When Siward, whofe prefaging heart
　　The caufe too well divin'd,
With agitated pleading look,
　　Rodolpho quickly join'd.

Now all retir'd ; a paufe enfu'd ;
　　To break it Siward try'd ;
Check'd by Rodolpho's look, which fpoke
　　Stern honour's-wounded pride.

At length he faid, " Let not my Lord
　　Sufpect a paffion bafe :
Did e'er my daughter's guiltlefs heart
　　With mean defire debafe ?

" A ruftick ftrippling at a jouft
　　With victory was crown'd,
And gain'd the bracelet, which is now
　　Entwin'd thy arm around.

　　　　　　　　　　　　" My

" My daughter's hand beftow'd the prize,
  But he audacious grew,
And dar'd, with bold prefumptuous love,
  Thy promis'd bride to view.

" I drove him from my wide domain,
  And many a year is paft,
Since in the wars of Paleftine
  I truft he breath'd his laft.

" But when Albina on thy arm
  The well-known bracelet view'd,
Her fhame and fcorn at Edgar's love
  Were painfully renew'd."

" There need no pleas, I reft affur'd,"
  Rodolpho anfwer'd mild;
" But this young Edgar, only once
  Did he behold thy child ?

" No plea of merit had the youth ?
  Was love his only claim ?"
He paus'd, and Siward's confcious cheek
  Confefs'd the blufh of fhame.

" His courage," Siward cried, " my lands
  From lawlefs ruffians fav'd;
But when I offer'd him reward,
  His pride the offer wav'd.

                           " Yet

" Yet till his manner, voice, and look,
　　His latent views exprefs'd,
Within my caftle he abode,
　　My brave acknowledg'd gueft."

Th' indignant Earl now check'd the tear
　　Which unpermitted ftole,
And to the rigour of his fate
　　Compos'd his manly foul.

" Go, o'er thy daughter's grief," he cried,
　　" Drop pity's foothing balm,
Whilft I in yon fequefter'd grove
　　Regain a mental calm."

But not the ftill fequefter'd grove
　　Could calm Rodolpho's foul,
Still on his mind Albina's tears
　　And Edgar's anguifh ftole.

Now beauty in the net of love
　　His heart clofe captive held;
Now grateful friendfhip's manlier force
　　The Syren's fnare repell'd.

" Did lefs of beauty, lefs of worth,
　　Around Albina blaze,
Lefs were the torture to refign,
　　But lefs would be the praife.

" For

" For this did Edgar from my head
   A certain death remove,
That I fhould fever from his breaft
   The laft faint hope of love?

" Did but his foul for fortune pant,
   Or fought he pow'r to gain,
How would I gratify each wifh!
   Yet ftill the fair retain.

" Retain the fair! retain her! how?
   What now her vows demand?
Know that another has her heart,
   Yet feize her captive hand?

" Forbid it, Pity! Honour, fcorn
   Indelible difgrace!
Love may with tortures tear my heart,
   But fhall not make it bafe."

He call'd a page :—to Edgar's houfe
   He bade him point the road:
Not diftant, in a graffy vale,
   Appear'd the plain abode.

A hawthorn hedge the garden bound,
   'Twas fill'd with many a flow'r;
A woodbine round a maple twin'd,
   Compos'd a fylvan bow'r.

                          And

And there the aged Orcar oft,
　　His talk of labour done,
Gaz'd on the spangled arch of heav'n,
　　And mus'd upon his son.

There too, that gallant son return'd,
　　He sought his griefs to calm ;
And pour'd upon the wounds of love
　　Confolatory balm.

" Ah ! whither, dear unhappy boy,
　　Does thy diſtraction tend?
Far ſwifter than yon ſailing clouds
　　Life haſtens to its end.

" Still as our ſteps, advancing, verge
　　On its declining ſtage,
The proſpects faint and diſtant grow
　　Which did our youth engage.

" Our paſſions, as we bend to earth,
　　Imbibe a ſombre gloom ;
And lengthening with our ſetting ſun,
　　The ſhadows reach the tomb.

" Then chief on thoſe who patient tread
　　An irkſome path of woe,
Bright burſting from a happier clime,
　　The ſtreams of glory flow.

" Nor.

" Nor urge *my* difappointed hopes,
  I do not *now* complain :
When I beheld thee, one embrace
  Repaid each former pain.

" I afk'd not for my darling wealth,
  Virtue was all my pray'r ;
And Heav'n did limit other gifts,
  To be more lavifh there.

" Yet, Edgar, if thy patient foul
  The taunt of pride repell'd, .
Patient endur'd the foldier's toil,
  Yet faw his rights withheld ;

" Oh ! bid it, in one trial more,
  Invulnerable prove,
And triumph o'er the envious fhaft
  Of difappointed Love."

" Envy ! Oh, father," cried the youth,
  " My heart the term difdains ;
That heart, where next, bright maid, to thee,
  The brave Rodolpho reigns.

" Had any fuitor crofs'd my hopes,
  With merit lefs replete,
I would have check'd his gay career,
  Or perifh'd at his feet.
                              " Father,

" Father, thou know'ſt Albina's face,
　Far lovelier was her mind;
While Siward favour'd, I full oft
　With her in converſe join'd.

" And ſtill the maid would tell the joys
　On virtuous love conferr'd;
Deceiv'd by ſanguine hope, I thought
　Her theme to me referr'd.

" Rodolpho now, with pureſt joy
　Shall liſten to that theme,
Feel each licentious wiſh confin'd,
　Yet taſte a bliſs ſupreme.

" For, him ſhe weaves the martial ſcarf:
　For him the garland wreathes:
Strikes at his call the ſoft-ton'd harp,
　And ſtrains ſoul-piercing breathes.

" Oh! let us ſeek ſome diſtant ſpot;
　My love I will ſupprefs;
The father, whom till now I griev'd,
　Henceforward I will bleſs.

" For thee, and thee alone, I'll ſtay
　The purpoſe of deſpair;
Conſcious that man is born to woe,
　Thoſe woes I'll firmly bear."

He faid, and with a fickly fmile
   The drooping Orcar cheer'd,
When fudden at the wicket gate
   The gen'rous Earl appear'd.

He faw his friend, a painful thrill
   Seem'd ev'ry thought to check,
'Till brave Rodolpho's outftretch'd arms
   Were circled round his neck.

Long paus'd the Earl, then fault'ring fpoke,
   " 'Twas much unkind to go,
To leave me on this awful day
   Did little friendfhip fhow.

" I come to lead thee to the hall,
   The feafts, the fports attend ;
And ev'n Albina's felf requefts
   The prefence of my friend."

" Does fhe requeft it ?" Edgar cry'd,
   And fix'd his glaring eye;
" She doth requeft it," faith the Earl,
   " Can'ft thou the fair deny ?"

" No, I will go!"—Forth from the bow'r
   With frantick fpeed he fprung;
His troubled foul to phrenfy'd rage
   By fancy'd wrong was ftung,

                     Now

Now whilſt upon his panting breaſt
   His mail he firmly ties,
Orcar on penſive Norfolk turn'd
   His mild perſuaſive eyes.

" Great Earl, ſhall not that youth's deſpair
   Thy kind concern engage?
He is my ſon, my only child,
   And lo! I droop with age."

" Oh venerable ſire! no wrong
   Thy Edgar ſhall annoy;
But follow, and prepare thy ſoul
   To meet a ſcene of joy."

Silent and ſwift acroſs the vale
   The tortur'd friends return'd;
Dejeƈtion ſunk Rodolpho's heart,
   With anger Edgar's burn'd.

" This low-born ſneer, this mean device,"
   Thus to himſelf he ſaid,
" Shall all her former virtues blaſt,
   And all her charms degrade.

" I thank her, for I now am free,
   My heart each fetter breaks;
'From viſions of ideal worth
   My wond'ring ſoul awakes.

H 2   " With

" With fmiles of cold contempt I'll meet
   Her proud exulting eye;
My heart may in the conflict break,
   But it fhall never figh."

Now broke upon his loathing view
   The caftle's turrets white;
Thofe turrets which in happier days
   Infpir'd a gay delight.

Far diff'rent now, each lofty fpire,
   And gaily fwelling dome,
Increas'd the horrors of defpair,
   And deepen'd all its gloom.

Now joyful, at the Earl's return,
   The portals were unbarr'd;
The bridal train in order ftood
   Within the caftle-yard.

Rodolpho fair Albina fought
   Within the hall of ftate;
Affrighted, trembling, and difmay'd,
   The mournful beauty fate.

Silent her father ftood, his looks
   Spake horror's pale prefage;
Ambition's fullen gloom, the fcowl
   Of difappointed rage.

Now

Now Edgar on his long-lov'd maid
    Throws his difdainful eyes;
But when he fees her grief of foul,
    Far diff'rent paffions rife.

" Thofe clafped hands, that folemn look,
    Do they infulting prove?
Thine, Norfolk, was the mean device,
    Thou tyrant in thy love!"

His trembling hand now grafps his fword,
    But honour, foon alarm'd,
Determines yet to fpare a foe,
    Unguarded and unarm'd.

" Yet, haughty Earl, the hour fhall come,
    Nor diftant is the time,
When, burfting from each vein, thy blood
    Shall expiate thy crime.

" 'Till then, with infolent delight
    My heartfelt anguifh view."
So thought the youth, and o'er his face
    His beaver fternly drew.

Radiant as in a night of froft
    Beams Cynthia's filver car,
Albina look'd, through chilling grief
    Each charm feem'd lovelier far.

Rodolphe

Rodolpho took one parting gaze,
A long and deep farewell;
It feem'd at once eternal love
And fix'd regret to tell.

Her father fciz'd her hand, fhe rofe,
To Norfolk's Earl fhe came;
Reluctant was her ling'ring ftep,
And terror fhook her frame.

" Can'ft thou," fhe cry'd, " the fudden pang,
Which reafon blam'd, forgive?
I never more fhall fee the youth,
Yet fuffer him to live."

The Earl receiv'd the proffer'd hand
That Siward had refign'd;
" Thou giveft her to me," he faid;
" I do," the Sire rejoin'd.

" Then thus with her I pay the debt
Which I to valour ow'd;"
He turn'd, and on his frantick friend
Th' angelick maid beftow'd.

Then whilft o'er all his glowing face
Benignant tranfport broke,
Thus to the agonized pair
The gen'rous Noble fpoke.

" Sweet

" Sweet mourner, turn, Rodolpho yields
　. To Edgar's claim, thy vows;
Turn, lovely maid, with tender fmiles
　　Now greet thy deftin'd fpoufe.

" Fortune and merit both combin'd,
　　Thy paffion fhall approve;
Nor thou, brave Edgar, doubt the friend
　　That gives thee e'en his love.

" Siward, if ftill thy narrow heart
　　Can humble worth difdain,
Know, Edgar from this hour is lord
　　Of many a fair domain.

" Soon o'er the lands which I beftow
　　His lib'ral care fhall fhine;
Give rapture to his father's heart,
　　And felf-reproach to thine.

" Nor, Edgar, let a friendly fear
　　Thy prefent blifs decreafe;
Approving virtue cheers my foul,
　　And all within is peace.

Charm'd by the joys which heav'n around
　　Benevolence hath thrown,
I fhare the bleffings I impart,
　　Nay, make them all my own.

　　　. . " Here-

" Hereafter in fome penfive hour
　　Should felfifh thoughts offend,
To banifh every mean regret,
　　I'll feek my happy friend.

" There as he fhines, in fortune, fame,
　　In love, in virtue bleft,
The mufick of his grateful voice
　　Shall harmonize my breaft."

Continuation of the 12th Chapter of THE
　　　　　GOSSIP'S STORY.

WHEN Sir William Milton had
finifhed the long manufcript, Captain Target, who had with great difficulty refrained
from paying his refpects to Morpheus during
the recital, began to roufe his faculties by
emphatical commendations, which he happily divided between the ftory and the reader.

Marianne, whofe eyes fwam with tears,
rejoiced that the lovers were at laft made
happy together, of which fhe had once many
doubts.

Mr.

Mr. Alfop applying every word which Marianne uttered in favour of love, to his own advantage, took courage, and ventured to give his opinion; which was, that it was very cleverly brought about to make my Lord give up fome demefnes to Edgar, for he thought the *Old Gentleman* never would have allowed his daughter to marry a man, who was not only of low birth, but who had no *fortune*.

"Mr. Alfop," faid Sir William contemptuoufly, "overlooks the circumftance which ennobled Edgar; he bore arms in Paleftine."

Captain Target could not fuffer a hint in favour of the military line to pafs unnoticed. He bowed profoundly to the Baronet, and declared himfelf happy in entertaining the fame honourable fentiments of the character of a foldier; adding in a theatrical ftyle, "None but the brave deferve the fair. Is not that your opinion, Mifs Dudley?"

"I hope, Sir," faid Louifa, colouring

at

at this unexpected reference, " I shall not offend your allowable partiality for your *own* profeffion by obferving, that I am glad Rodolpho is not left unhappy. Indeed I think he is placed in the moft enviable fituation, fince the confcioufnefs of having performed a highly generous action, muft afford a perfect delight to an exalted mind. But Edgar labours under the weight of an obligation, which he never can repay ; befides, he may fear that his tranfports are the caufe of diftreffing his benefactor."

" My fentiments, Madam, refpecting the fublime pleafures of generofity entirely coincide with yours," faid Sir William ; " but I am forry to hear you fpeak of gratitude as a *painful* fenfation."

" Not abfolutely fo," replied Louifa, diftreft at an obfervation which was accompanied by a look of angry penetration. " I only think Rodolpho's is the moft enviable lot. He is placed in fuch a favourable point of view that had I been Albina, I

fhould

fhould have felt half forry to refign fuch a
worthy lover."

"Not if you had been previoufly attached to Edgar, fifter, and recollected what he
had fuffered for your fake," faid the gentle
Marianne. "True, Madam," exclaimed
Alfop with a deep figh; "but every body
don't know what true love is."

"Indeed, fifter," returned Louifa, laughing, "Mr. Alfop is a better adept in love
affairs than I am : but let us change the fubject of converfation. It grows too interefting."

Mr. Dudley now obferved, that if the
manufcript had entertained his friends, it
anfwered the purpofe for which he had introduced it. Its merit, he faid, confifted in
its fimplicity, and he was going to make fome
obfervations on the ftudied ornaments with
which many modern poets overload their
productions, till they obfcure the fenfe, and
difturb the harmony of the language; when
the entrance of a fervant to announce fupper

hap-

happily relieved the Danbury gentlemen from a literary difcuffion, of which, to fay the truth, they were not very fond.

On their return home, Mr. Alfop afked his friend's opinion refpecting the prefent ftate of his affairs. The Captain fwore they were in an admirable train, and mentioned Louifa's laughing at him, as a convincing proof that fhe was apprehenfive of his influence over her fifter's mind.

In fhort, things were thought ripe for the grand attack, and it was agreed that a letter fhould be written expreffive of Mr. Alfop's paffion, which his confident promifed to deliver. They then feparated for the evening; the Captain to fabricate a fpeech, intimating a ftruggle between love and friendfhip; and Mr. Alfop to read the Polite Letter-writer, prior to the compofition of his intended epiftle.

CHAP. XIII.

A letter (but not the one the reader was in-
duced to hope for) calls forth some very
antiquated notions.

THE poft arrived at Stannadine foon
after the departure of the vifitors, and Mr.
Dudley, on receiving a packet from his London
correfpondent, wifhed his daughters a
good night, and retired to his chamber.

The intelligence it contained was of the
unpleafant kind. It certified the report, that
the French had detached a fquadron to lay
wait for the Weft-India fleet, which was deftitute of adequate means of defence againft
an unexpected attack; it alfo added, that the
capture of a fhip in which they had hoped to
receive large remittances, had precipitated
the ruin of Mr. Tonnereau's firm, which
had that day ftopped payment.

While Mr. Dudley fat meditating on his
misfortunes, with the deep regret of a man

fen-

fenfible that he had been guilty of an irretrievable error, Louifa entered the room.
Mr. Dudley's agitated mind was ftrongly im-
preffed on his countenance; but his daughter was in too much diforder to regard it.
Pale, trembling, and unable to fpeak, fhe
gave him a letter which *fhe* had juft received;
and while he perufed it, fhe funk into a chair.
I fhall copy this alarming epiftle :

       ‘ TO MISS DUDLEY.

    ‘ Madam,

   ‘ I make bold, though a perfeſt ftranger,
‘ to trefpafs upon your goodnefs.   I am
‘ told that you are fhortly to be married to
‘ Sir William Milton.   I muft fay, Madam,
‘ for all I have heard of you, I wifh you a
‘ better hufband than fuch a villain.   . I am a
‘ poor widow woman, who keeps a coffee-
‘ houfe in —— ftreet, and a few years ago
‘ my daughter (a very handfome, well-be-
‘ haved young woman) went to the Indies,
‘ in hopes to make her fortune.   She there
‘ met Sir William, then only Captain Milton,
                         ‘ and

' and he fell in love with her, and fhe with
' him.   He promifed to marry her, and fo
' at laft ruined her.   But he kept her like a
' Princefs all the while fhe ftaid there.   Poor
' creature, the worfe for her now.   For at
' laft he quarrelled with her, and left her be-
' hind him when he came to England, and
' would do nothing for her, and fhe is come
' home in great diftrefs indeed.   She has two
' children, Madam, and I have hard work
' to maintain myfelf thefe bad times.   So I
' hope you will perfuade Sir William to do
' fomething handfome, and I fhall be bound
' to pray for you; from

' Your humble fervant,

' MARY MORTON.

' N. B. He ought to do fomething for his
' children, they are too young to affront him."

Mr. Dudley, after perufing the letter, caft
his eyes upon his daughter, and afked her
what could be done.

"Can I, Sir," faid Louifa, burfting into
tears, "vow to love and to honour a man
who

who labours under such an imputation ? Cruelty is added to licentious perfidy. My dear father, forgive me! My very foul revolts againſt this union."

" Oh worthy of thy excellent mother," ſaid Mr. Dudley: " No, Louiſa, you cannot. I am far from thinking ſo lightly as ſome people do of the vicious irregularities in which many young men indulge : but to abandon the unhappy creature he has ſeduced, to the horrors and temptations of poverty; to make no proviſion for his innocent, helpleſs offspring! Rather would I ſee thee a beggar, than ſuffer thee to contaminate thyſelf by participating in his guilty affluence. He capable of a generous affection! Impoſſible !"

" You have relieved my anxiety," replied Miſs Dudley ; " yet why ſhould I doubt that my dear father would ſee the atrocity of ſuch an action in as ſtrong a light as myſelf? But, Sir, you have had letters from London. Not diſtreſſing ones I hope."

" They

" They are not consolatory, my child,"
resumed Mr. Dudley; " but we muft firft
decide upon this affair."

Louisa, who perceived her father agitated
by a contrariety of paffions, gueffed at the
intelligence he would not communicate, and
regretted that fhe had rufhed into his prefence, to overwhelm him with the additional
weight of her own forrows. She ftrove to
compofe herfelf, and again perufed the letter
from Mrs. Morton. She began to think it
poffible fhe might have been betrayed by her
fecret prejudices, to adopt a fevere opinion
without fufficient proofs; and, determined
not to truft to her own judgment, afked her
father, if the letter did not bear evident
marks of being dictated by ftrong refentment.

Had Mr. Dudley feen what paffed in his
daughter's mind at that moment, he would
have contemplated the triumph of filial piety,
defirous of giving up every thing but its integrity, to ward the fhafts of misfortune from
him.

him. He would have admired the virtue
that warred with even the innocent and allowable propenfities of the heart, and ftill
more would his daughter's charaĉter have
rifen in his eye, from her attempt to hide the
intended facrifice from his obfervation, by
giving to the excufes fhe was forming, the air
of extenuating love. He was ignorant of
thefe circumftances, and when Louifa afked
him, if it would not at leaft be juft to allow
Sir William an opportunity of juftifying his
conduĉt, he fuppofed it poffible the diflike
his daughter at firft expreffed againft her
lover, had fubfided; and was fucceeded by
a degree of attachment.

But fince love, though indulged to the
degree of dotage, would not, in Mr. Dudley's opinion, obviate the many evils incident in an alliance between a virtuous woman and a profligate man; he only wifhed,
from the fuppofed ftate of Louifa's affections, that Sir William might be able to juftify himfelf from the fevere imputations caft
upon

upon his chara&er. On reading the letter again, he thought it probable that fpleen, violence, and difappointment might aggravate the offence. "But depend upon it, my love," faid he, "the charge has fome foundation. It would be wrong not to hear what he can plead in his defence, and indeed you cannot now decline his addreffes, without giving him a reafon for your condu&. I will fpeak to him to-morrow morning."

Louifa now preffed her father to difcover the purport of his intelligence from London, but he eluded inquiry, determined that fhe fhould know nothing more of his misfortunes, till Mrs. Morton's accufation was either refuted or confirmed. He rightly thought, that though pecuniary circumftances may influence a woman's choice, when no folid obje&ions can be made to the lover; innocence, if bribed by the wealth of the univerfe, fhould fhrink from a conne&ion with vice. He therefore pretended the eafe he did not feel, and reminding her of the

latenefs

latenefs of the hour, with a fervent carefs difmiffed her to repofe. It was a bleffing which neither of them enjoyed that night: befides the preffure of their own forrows, each of them laboured under the apprehenfion of what the other endured; for the filial and paternal ties are at leaft as fufceptible of thefe emotions, as either friendfhip or love.

C H A P. XIV.

A wealthy lover is difmiffed by a family upon the eve of bankruptcy, for what the world may ftyle fpirited conduct.

MISS Dudley rifing early next morning, as was her ufual cuftom, to fuperintend domeftick affairs, met Sir William in the paffage leading to the breakfaft-room. He had an unufual degree of urbanity in his afpect, and feizing her hand with an air of gallantry, begged the favour of a few minutes' converfation; Louifa reluctantly affented; and he gave her a letter he had juft received

from

from his mother, in which her Ladyſhip expreſſed her eagerneſs to receive a daughter of
her late beloved friend, in a yet *more* en-
dearing point of view, than that in which her
nephew hoped to have preſented one.   She
concluded with begging, that his amiable miſtreſs would ſacrifice a few ſcruples of punc-
tilio to her earneſt intreaties.   Her health,
ſhe ſaid, was apparently declining, and ſhe
felt all a parent's anxiety to ſee the happineſs
of her ſon ſecured, and to participate in his
tranſports, while ſhe was yet able to enjoy
them.   Sir William ſtrengthened this argument by urging his own impatience; he flat-
tered himſelf he had not been wholly unde-
ſerving her favour; ſettlements he was ready
to diſcuſs with Mr. Dudley; but as he meant
by their liberality to prove his high ſenſe of
her merits, no objections could ariſe on that
head.   He concluded with hoping, that as
female coquetry had no part in her character,
ſhe would ſhorten the time of probation, and
favour him with an early day.

Louiſa,

Louisa, with streaming eyes, perused Lady
Milton's letter, and from the maternal ten-
derness visible in every part, was led to wish
that she could gratify the kind request. She
started from her reverie at Sir William's last
words; the proof of his unworthiness flashed
upon her mind, and while her soul over-
flowed with veneration for the mother, it
shrunk in abhorrence from her son. She
attempted to speak, but was unable. She
turned aside her face glowing with confu-
sion, and clung to the arm of her chair as if
to support her trembling frame. Sir William, who construed her behaviour into
maiden delicacy, was going, by declarations
of everlasting love, to deliver her from her
embarrassment; when Mr. Dudley entered
the room. Louisa never beheld her father
approach with more pleasure; she instantly
rose, and referring her lover to him for an
explanation, hastily withdrew.

Though the young Baronet would have
preferred receiving from his mistress the desired

fired confent, he was not thrown into defpair
by this reference. He gave Mr. Dudley his
mother's letter, and informed him that he
had been urging Mifs Dudley to favour him
with a fpeedy union. Lady Milton's confent was, he faid, of no confequence in one
point of view, as his fortune was perfectly
independent, and in his own poffeffion; but
as it implied a juft refpect for the Lady he
fo highly efteemed, he could not but rejoice
in every tribute that was paid to his Louifa's
virtues.

Mr. Dudley, after obferving that he was
the laft man upon earth to whom apologies
for filial deference were neceffary, declared
his grateful fenfe of Lady Milton's favourable
fentiments of his family. He then hinted,
that before the propofed alliance could take
place, a very painful fubject muft be difcuffed.

Sir William, fuppofing he meant fettle-
ments, replied, that in all pecuniary concerns, Mifs Dudley's wifhes fhould be the
only bound to his liberality.

"I do

" I do not doubt your generofity on that head, Sir William: it was to another circumftance I alluded. But let me premife, that you fee before you a man of bankrupt fortunes; one who has ruined himfelf and his child by a fatal confidence; one who has nothing but his integrity left. Be pleafed, Sir, in our future converfation to remember this circumftance."

Sir William, grafping Mr. Dudley's hand, protefted the intelligence gave him no pain except upon his account. He would with pleafure afford him all the affiftance which his ample fortune could beftow. He would fettle upon him what income he fhould judge neceffary for his fupport; and as to his Louifa, the enjoyments of wealth would be doubled to him by her confenting to fhare them. He thanked Heaven he had no occafion to bound his expences by parfimonious rules, and liberality was the darling paffion of his foul.

Mr.

Mr. Dudley bowed with the air of one who would rather avoid than court the favour of proud munificence. Anxious, however, to avoid offending the haughty youth he, intended to reprove, he exprefſed a lively fenſe of his generous promiſes. " Indulge me, Sir," faid he, " with the privilege our preſent fituation claims, and fuffer me not only to act the part of a father to my girl, but of a real friend to you. A report has reached us which has given us both pain; and a juſt regard for Louiſa's future peace compels me to afk the nature of your connexion with Miſs Morton ?"

A ſtroke of electricity could not have more fenſibly affected Sir William Milton. A deep ſuffuſion ſtole over his gloomy features, which was ſoon ſucceeded by a livid paleneſs. There needed no ſkill in phyſiognomy to exclaim, " Guilty, upon mine honour."

Mr. Dudley, who hoped his ſilence was at

leaſt

leaft a proof of contrition, proceeded : " It is not my wifh, Sir, further to diftrefs you; I fee and pity your confufion. Few of us can walk in the unerring path of rectitude; and perhaps a fincere endeavour to reclaim our wandering fteps is all that can be expected from human infirmity. Though licentious indulgencies ever were and muft be criminal, I am willing to allow fomething for the impetuofity of youthful paffions; the influence of diffipated fociety; and the unreftrained freedom of manners in which Europeans indulge themfelves, in the luxurious climate of the Eaft. But there are fome circumftances in the diftreffing account which fhocks credibility, and I doubt not but you will exculpate yourfelf from *them*."

" Name them," faid Sir William, in an imperious accent.

" That you have abandoned the unhappy creature you feduced, to want and all its horrid temptations. Nay, that you have
neglected

neglected to provide for your own helplefs, unoffending offspring."

" You muft give up the author of this report," refumed the Baronet, in a loud, authoritative tone.

" Not till you in a fatisfactory manner refute the charge."

" I fcorn to anfwer anonymous fcandal," faid Sir William. " If you efteem me a villain on flender proofs—retain your opinion."

" I fhould rejoice in your vindication; but this warmth is no ftep towards it. The confequences of my thinking you a villain, is my daughter's rejection of your addrefs."

" You fpeak, Mr. Dudley, as if the obligations were on *your* fide. I have a due fenfe of your daughter's merit; but love has not fo blinded my reafon as to make me undervalue my own pretenfions."

" I perceive, Sir," faid Mr. Dudley, " that you *remember* my poverty: but I am ftill rich in my child, nor dare I intruft you with my only remaining treafure, till I am affured

I com-

I commit her to the protection of a man of principle and honour. You frown, Sir; I cannot be silenc'd by a frown. The man who can so far preserve his equanimity of mind during the ruin of his fortune, as to ask nothing of the wealthy, is too rich to fear their resentment."

" Did you, Mr. Dudley, formerly find this intellectual wealth a good marketable commodity?" interrogated Sir William. " I rather suspect you did not fully appreciate its value, till you retired from mercantile pursuits."

" If by reminding me of the profession I once followed, you mean to throw any reflection on the general character of a British merchant, you rather expose your own want of information respecting the resources and wealth of this empire, than discredit me. I glory in having stimulated the industry of thousands; increased the natural strength of my country; and enlarged her revenue and reputation, as far as a private individual could.

could. My fall has not been accelerated by vice, extravagance, or dishonesty: but we wander from the point. Disputes of this nature are only unnecessary aggravations. If you continue to refuse the desired explanation, I can no longer consider you as Louisa's lover; and whatever my sentiments of your conduct may be, it is only in that character that I can claim any right to inquire into it."

" I question," said Sir William, " if *that character* gives you the right to which you pretend. But it is not from *you*, Sir, that I shall take my dismission. I must see Miss Dudley, I will know how far you have prejudiced her against me. She may perhaps explain *your* motives for this extraordinary interference."

" I have no improper ones," replied Mr. Dudley, rising to ring the bell. Then addressing the servant who came in, he desired that Louisa would immediately attend. The gentlemen remained sullenly silent till she entered the room.

" My

"My dear," faid Mr. Dudley, "Sir William Milton wifhes to fpeak to you, perhaps he will favour you with the explanation he has refufed me." He then attempted to withdraw; Louifa fixed her pleading eyes upon him, as if intreating his ftay; but he determined to refift their filent language; till Sir William obferved that he had nothing to urge to Mifs Dudley which it was improper for her father to hear.

"I find, Madam," faid the haughty lover, "that I have forfeited Mr. Dudley's efteem. I wifh to know if *you* too confider me as a bafe feducer; the betrayer of innocence; one who meanly abandons the creature he has plunged into guilt: nay, who deferts his own helplefs, unoffending offspring? Are you too, Madam, refolved to withhold from me the name of my accufer?"

"If my father," replied Louifa, "has informed you of the charge, you muft know in what light I confider it. I fhould defert the female charaġer if I was deftitute of delicacy
and

and compaſſion: and unleſs you wiſh to *diſ-prove* theſe cenſures, of what uſe can it be to diſcover from whence they proceed?"

" I perceive," returned Sir William, " (I wiſh I could ſay with indifference,) the ſlender hold I have of your affeﬅions. Perhaps, Madam, it was the ſplendour of my offers alone that procured me *even* a momentary attention."

" Had you, Sir, appeared to me at firſt in the light you now do, not even your *ſplendid* offers would have excited a moment's heſitation. I cannot reconcile my heart to an huſband deficient in moral principle."

" And may I aſk," exclaimed the peremptory lover, " what that high ſtandard of perfeﬅion is by which thoſe who aſpire to you muſt be meaſured?"

" The ſtandard after which you inquire, Sir William, does not exceed moderation: it is humble like my own deſerts. But we only agitate each other; permit me to withdraw."

"No, by my foul, I cannot lofe you!" cried Sir William, in violent emotion. He would have bent his knee, but recollecting that Mr. Dudley was prefent, refrained from the undue condefcenfion. He gazed upon her a few moments, and then in a low tone faid, " You could not treat me with this indifference if you ever loved me. But even at this moment you fcornfully enjoy my agony."

" As thefe cenfures," refumed Mifs Dudley, " are merely intended to evade a charge you do *not* deny, I need not labour to reinftate myfelf in *your* good opinion. Yet I could wifh to preferve Lady Milton's, and will intreat as a *laft* favour, that, when you inform her of what has paffed, you will give as candid an account of me as can confift with your own vindication."

" Sovereign contempt, by Heaven! But, Madam, you miftake me if you think to awe me into fupplicatory fubmiffion. However highly you may rate my love, I can borrow fome of your philofophy to conceal its pangs.

May

May you find a worthier lover, or at leaft
one who is a better adept in the difguifes of
courtfhip."

Sir William then ordered his horfes, and
Mr. Dudley, after an invitation to ftay
breakfaft, which was coolly declined, did
not oppofe his departure.

CHAP. XV.

Calamity frequently expands a generous heart.

MR. Dudley attempted to fortify his
daughter's mind with thofe principles, which
not only blunt the keeneft arrows of difappointment, but convert them into bleffings.
" Your dream of happinefs, my love," faid
he, " appears to be terminated: yet from the
calm confiftency of your conduct, I truft
you are not deftitute of thofe mental fup-
ports, without which all that the world calls
good is but fplendid mifery. You feel, my
Louifa, that you have acted as you ought,
and that reflection will enable you to fupport·

I 5   even·

even the painful difcovery of the unworthi-
nefs of a favoured lover." " It was your recommendation, Sir," replied Louifa, " which
firft induced me to accept Sir William Milton's offers. I relied upon your judgment,
and felt affured that the good qualities you
afcribed to him would excite my efteem, my
gratitude, and my love. I have every reafon to rejoice that we have been convinced
of the defects in his temper and conduct, before it became my painful duty to endure
them. But I fear, my dear father, that the
termination of this connection may be of ferious confequences to you?"

" When your mother died," replied Mr.
Dudley, " I loft my high relifh for the comforts and pleafures affluence beftows. I truft
my heart has not been tainted by mifanthro-
py, but I have been fo accuftomed to feek
for my pleafures and comforts out of my own
mind, that to renounce fociety, and to feclude
myfelf from the world, will fcarcely excite a
figh upon my own account. For you, my
child,

child, I deeply feel; your fpirits have not
been broken by repeated trials, and, rifing
into life, you look upon it with all the fanguine preference of youth.   Anxious to preferve to you the profperity you have hitherto
enjoyed, I confidered Sir William's apparent generofity with too favourable an eye;
but no more of him.   Amidft the ruin of
my fortunes, I rejoice that the little eftate
your grandfather left you in Lancafhire for
pocket-money will preferve you from indi-
gence.   You have not to thank me for this
referve, it was happily fecured from my in-
difcretion, and confequently could not be fa-
crificed to an artful, ungenerous friend."

"My dearest father," faid Mifs Dudley,
" do not afflict me by thefe felf-upbraidings.
I owe you a debt I never can difcharge.
Not to mention the thoufand kind attentions
which have hitherto made my life a round of
delights, it is from you I have received a fuperior education; you inftilled into my in-
fant foul principles which, unlefs my own

fault, muſt inſure my preſent and future happineſs. Why, Sir, for I will ſpeak proudly, fhould not *your* daughter be able to find pleaſure and comfort in the reſources of her own mind as well as yourſelf? We ſhall live very comfortably upon that dear little eſtate you talk of. I always had a turn for œconomy and management; am quite a cottager in my heart, I aſſure you. The few friends we poſſeſs will continue to eſteem us in any ſtation; and as to general acquaintance, I never conſidered them important to my happineſs."

" A cottage life, my love," reſumed Mr. Dudley, " is not ſo pleaſant in reality as in theory. Like every other ſtate it has its vexations, even for thoſe who were born with no higher hopes. To them who have been accuſtomed to the elegant enjoyments of life, it preſents evils that patience and fortitude may teach us to ſupport; but which are doubtleſs evils. To you they will be

lefs

lefs painful than to a light frivolous mind, and this is all my confolation."

Mr. Dudley then afked if Marianne had been informed of his perplexities? Louifa anfwered in the negative; but owned that her fifter had lately made fome inquiries to which (from an idea that it would be moft agreeable to her father) fhe had given eva- five anfwers.

Mr. Dudley commended her prudence. " When your grandmother took Marianne," faid he, " it was with the exprefs condition that fhe fhould exclufively be confidered as *her* child. I truft you poffefs her friend-fhip, and will occafionally receive fubftantial proofs of it: yet to be wholly caft as a dependant upon her bounty would not, I think, contribute to the happinefs of either. She is dutiful, affectionate, and generous; but her feelings are peculiarly lively; and, as is the cafe with moft people of ftrong fenfibility, there is fome degree of uncertainty in her conduct. For my own part, there is

scarcely

fcarcely a mifery I would not fooner endure, than penfion myfelf upon my child,
with an apprehenfion that by fo doing I
might prevent her from forming fuch connexions as her fortune and merit might
otherwife attract. Had Mr. Pelham been
agreeable to her, I think I could have been
happy in the protection of fuch a fon. I
have judged from her caft of character, that
a fingle life would be moft conducive to her
happinefs; but as even candour itfelf could
hardly acquit me of interefted views, were I
to urge fuch advice in my prefent fituation,
I have only to hope that I fhall be able to
conceal from her the prefent ftate of my affairs, until fhe felects fome worthy admirer
for her hufband. Our expences at Stannadine indeed are confiderable, yet I think
continuing them a few months longer, from
the hope of her forming a fuitable attachment, is juftifiable. I fhall not fcruple applying to her for a fhare of them; befides,
my love, (here Mr. Dudley faintly fmiled,)
                                                        perhaps

perhaps a publick enemy may prove more favourable to me than an infidious friend."

Mifs Dudley acquiefced in thefe opinions, and Marianne foon joined the party, anxious to know the caufe of Sir William Milton's hafty departure. Her father was happy to hear her, after the perufal of Mrs. Morton's letter, exprefs ftrong deteftation of libertine principles; a fentiment which, I will affirm, is natural to a delicate unvitiated female mind.

Mr. Dudley then informed his daughters, that fome unexpected bufinefs would call him to London. He lamented that he fhould lofe the fociety which was fo delightful to him; but yet would not be fo felfifh as to defire them to refign the country, while glowing in the richeft robe of fummer, to accompany him to a dirty, deferted town. Louifa guefling at her father's real motives for declining their company, acquiefced in the pretended one: and Marianne was too much enamoured with purling ftreams, and mofs-grown dells, to endure the thought of leaving Stannadine.   CHAP.

CHAP. XVI.

*An interefting adventure. The purblind God
of Love difpatched upon two different
errands, commits an irreparable miftake.*

THE interefting particulars I have
been relating afforded the greateft treat to
my neighbours that they had enjoyed for
many years. Two lovers at firft encouraged, then haftily difmiffed, opened a fine
field for conjecture. Curiofity, which had
hitherto been employed in fucceffively de-
tecting the extravagance, parfimony, carelefs
negligence, and fufpicious watchfulnefs of
Mifs Dudley's domeftic management, was
entirely diverted from family arrangements,
to confider what *could* be the caufe of
thefe revolutions. After many debates, we
at laft finally determined, that Mifs Marianne refufed Mr. Pelham, becaufe her father

ther gave him a bad character; and that Sir
William Milton *flew* off, when he difcovered Louifa had no fortune.

The frequent vifits of Captain Target and
Mr. Alfop to Stannadine were another inex-
hauftible topic of converfation. I obferved
that this fummer had proved the healthieft I
had ever known. None of my friends anfwered my inquiries with complaints of
feeling they did *not know how:* not one
creature had a nervous attack or was out of
fpirits. Sometimes we difpatched a noble-
man in a coach and four to fetch off Marianne, and then again created a group of bai-
liffs, armed with an execution, to drive out
the whole family. For my own part, I
made a very prudential ufe of this general
folicitude. Whenever I laboured under any
of thofe little perplexities which miftreffes of
a family fometimes feel, I introduced the
Dudleys, and can truly fay, that more than
once it prevented my party from difcovering
that my coffee was cold, and my filver waiter
dreadfully tarnifhed. My

My friendſhip for Miſs Cardamum would have given me pain, on account of the evident dereliction of her beaux; but happily that lady had accompanied her papa to Scarborough, from whence ſhe wrote very ſprightly letters to Mrs. Medium, obliquely intimating, that ſhe had danced with two of the firſt gentlemen of faſhion there, who had ſaid very *ſoft* things to her. She inquired with perfect *nonchalance*, whether Alſop or Target had run away with Marianne Dudley yet; declaring either of them were very likely to draw in a raw young creature, who had ſeen nothing of the world. I conſidered theſe obſervations as an unqueſtionable proof that they had totally forfeited my good opinion.

I am however willing to hope that the reader's regard is not ſo wholly withdrawn from them, but that curioſity is ſtill anxious to know the event of the letter, which we left Mr. Alſop compoſing in the twelfth chapter. It was indeed a very unfortunate performance, for though

written

written in a fair legible hand, and very cor-
rectly fpelt, it was fo long in finifhing, that
before it was ready to prefent, Mr. Dudley
had fet out for London. As it began with
ftating, that the reafon which determined
him to that mode of addrefs was to avoid the
jealous attention of her father, the very ba-
fis on which it was founded being fubverted,
the unhappy edifice fell to the ground: and
thus the offspring of the Loves and Graces
was fmothered in its birth. But ftill the
heroick Alfop was not difcouraged. How
perfevering and indefatigable is love!

To account for the confidence which
fwelled his hopes, I muft difclofe a fecret
which my Betty told me; namely, that by
means of Mifs Lappel, the milliner, a fecret
correfpondence had been entered into between the afpiring lover and Mrs. Patty.
Every one who has clandeftinely addreffed
a rich heirefs knows that it is of great confequence to fecure the waiting-maid; and I
would not be fo refpectful to Mr. Alfop's
learning,

learning, as to hint that he was deficient in fuch neceffary knowledge. Mrs. Patty's zeal to have her lady married was too warm to be very nice about the intended hufband; and no fooner did Mifs Lappel tell her how deeply Mr. Alfop was *fmitten*, and how very rich he was, than Patty thought it might do very well. They agreed indeed that he was *no wit*, and rather flow in converfation; but then he was good-natured, and Patty obferved with a wink, that the *fharpeft* men did not make the beft hufbands. In fine; by a prudent difpofal of a few yards of Valenciennes edging, Mr. Alfop fecured an able affiftant, and Patty entertained her lady with encomiums upon that gentleman's great merit, as often as fhe dared to enter upon the fubject. The trufty Abigail too, whenever fhe wanted a little article at Mifs Lappel's, took care to tell the happy lover, that her lady feemed more and more pleafed when fhe told her about him, and that fhe was fure it would *do* in time,

Relying

Relying upon this intelligence, and feeling
a degree of fufpicion whether his old friend
Target would play fair, for which doubt, to
fay truth, he had fome reafon, Mr. Alfop
determined to truft all to his own perfon and
eloquence; therefore, one fine hot morning
in July, he fet out, like another Paris, to
conquer or die.   Not, indeed, attired like
the young Trojan, when he challenged the
gruff, ill-behaved King of Sparta to the lifts
of war; but in clean filk ftockings; and a
new pink padufuay waiftcoat; his hair load-
ed with powder; and the lower part of his
face fo enveloped in an enormous beau
dafh, as to threaten fuffocation.   He wore
a large bouquet of myrtles and geraniums,
whether with an emblematick defign, I will
not fay, and toffing a light rat-tan in his
right hand, tripped nimbly over the meadow.
I do not compare him to any ancient god,
or modern knight of chivalry, not recollecting any fimilitude juft in point.   As he
walked along he meditated, and determined

to

to tell Mifs Marianne, that he thought her
the prettieft creature in the world; and that
if fhe did not pity him, death muft be the
inevitable confequenee: when, lo! as he
turned round a corner to enter the court
gate, fhe burft upon his view—not fitting
alone in a fhady bower—not gracefully reclined upon the turf, with a book in her
hand, the emblem of elegant fcience; not
awakening the echoes with her melodious
voice; but pale, agitated, difordered in her
look and appearance.   She had juft alighted
from a carriage which ftood at the gate, and
by the affiftance of two gentlemen, who
feemed abforbed in their attention to their
fair charge, flowly entered the houfe.   Mr.
Alfop's alarm banifhed from his mind his
intended heroicks, and he haftily inquired
of a fervant the caufe of this incident.—He
was informed that Mifs Marianne had rid-
den out that morning, and narrowly efcaped a dreadful accident.   Her horfe had
taken fright at a carriage which fhe met
                                   upon

upon the road, and run away with her. She had fufficient prefence of mind to keep her feat, till a young gentleman who followed the carriage, with equal agility and dexterity ſtopped the terrified animal, and extricated her from her perilous ſituation. The alarm however had overpowered her fpirits, and ſhe repeatedly fainted. Her preferver placed her in the chaiſe with his father, and both of them humanely accompanied her home. Mr. Alſop, judging his fuit could not commence that morning, left his compliments, and after a great deal of ſorrow for the accident, and joy that ſhe was not hurt, promiſed to call again the next day.

Miſs Dudley met her fiſter with tender anxiety, and affiſted her to her chamber. As foon as ſhe was affured that ſhe had received no real injury, ſhe left her to calm her agitated fpirits, and returned to thank the gentlemen, for having preferved a
life

life fo truly valuable. The elder of the two, who feemed near fixty, had a keen, fenfible afpe&; the other did not appear to exceed twenty, and was remarkably handfome.

When Louifa had fatisfied their concern, by informing them, that her fifter was already much calmer, the elder of the gentlemen declared, that if the lady did not fuffer from her alarm, he fhould almoft be fo felfifh as to rejoice in a circumftance which had accelerated his introdu&ion to a family, of whom he had conceived the higheft opinion. He then faid his name was Clermont, that he had lately arrived at a feat he had in the vicinity, and fhould be happy to be confidered, by the Dudleys, in the light of a neighbour and a friend.

Louifa, who had heard Captain Target mention a Lord Clermont, with whom he was upon a moft familiar footing, rightly concluded her prefent vifitor to be that noblemrn. She replied, that fhe felt

assured

affured her father (who was then from home)
would be happy to cultivate an acquaintance
fo much to their honour. Mr. Clermont
then requefted permiffion to call and inquire
after the lady's health next morning, which
fhe readily granted, and the gentlemen withdrew, highly pleafed with the exquifite beauty of Marianne, and the graceful politenefs
of her fifter.

Mifs Dudley now inquired of Marianne
the circumftances of her late alarm, and was
happy to fee her recovered from every ill effect of it. She then told her what had paffed in the drawing-room, the rank of the family, their wifh to commence an acquaintance, the ftriking countenance of Lord
Clermont, and the expreffive beauty of his
fon. This latter circumftance Marianne de-
nied, for poffibly her fright prevented her
from obferving him; fhe alfo feemed to
think there would be an impropriety in receiving a vifit from him during her father's
abfence. Louifa laughed at her fifter's pru-

dery,

dery, till Marianne was rather difpleafed, and pettifhly anfwered, that as fhe was determined upon a fingle life, her error was merely characteriftick and of no confequence. She appeared, however, next morning dreffed in an uncommonly elegant defhabille, and her natural charms were improved by the advantage of well-adapted, but apparently, unftudied ornament. I would not have my readers from thence conclude, that fhe was not really difpleafed at Mifs Dudley's indifcreet permiffion; or that her refolution in favour of " bleffed finglenefs " faultered; no, young lady wifhes to be feen a " mere figure," and a perfon may be very angry at their heart, and yet adorn their face with an enchanting fmile.

Mr. Clermont was accompanied by his fifter, a girl about fourteen, whom he prefented to the ladies; as one zealoufly defirous to obtain their favourable opinion. He interrupted Marianne's thanks for the affiftance he fo fortunately gave her, by expref-

fing

fing the tranfport he felt at being able to render it.   Mifs Dudley directed her attention to Mifs Clermont, who being too young and too timid to join much in converfation, it was principally fupported by her brother and Marianne.   Never was fuch a wonderful coincidence of opinion!   Both were paffionate admirers of the country; both loved moonlight walks, and the noife of diftant waterfalls; both were enchanted by the found of the fweet-toned harp, and the almoft equally foft cadence of the paftoral and elegiack mufe; in fhort, whatever was paffionate, elegant, and fentimental in art; or beautiful, penfive, and enchanting in nature.

When minds are in fuch happy unifon, time flies unperceived.   I cannot guefs how long the morning call might have been protracted, had not the appearance of Mr. Alfop excited a different train of ideas.   His drefs and manner were equally calculated to caricature the part he meant to perform; and the hopes Mrs. Patty infpired had banifhed his natural timidity, without fubftituting

any

any thing more valuable. His whole behaviour put the politeneſs of the party to a ſe-
vere teſt. Marianne bit her lips to avoid
laughing at his ſolemn inquiries reſpecting
the conſequences of her fright, and his aſſurances of the pain he felt at hearing of it.
Mr. Clermont could only anſwer with a bow,
when he aſſumed the office of Ciceroni, by
offering to conduct him to all the *pretty places* in the garden. Miſs Dudley's embarraſſ-
ment was increaſed, by obſerving that Miſs
Clermont had by no means obtained a command over her riſible muſcles; but ſat pinch-
ing her fingers to prevent a loud laugh. The
Danbury Adonis determined when he left
home, to *ſit out* any company that might be
at Stannadine; for to ſay truth he was tired
of hot morning walks, and determined to
carry off the prize before the return of her
father. The Clermonts, therefore, were
compelled to order their carriage, and while
the ladies accompanied them to the door,
Miſs Clermont expreſſed a hope that though
her mother was not then in the country, Miſs
Dudleys

Dudleys would have the goodnefs to excufe her abfence, and favour them with their company at the park. Louifa, fearful of offending her fifter's prudence, poftponed the invitation till Mr. Dudley's return.

Mr. Alfop, who confidered this vifit as no good omen for him, felt his difagreeable prognofticks confirmed, by Louifa's returning to him with a flight apology for her fifter's abfence. He did not doubt that fhe was playing the part of a Duenna, and defpairing to elude fuch a watchful Argus, at one time refolved boldly to demand a conference with his charmer. But recollecting that it would be as prudent to try to propitiate her keeper, he frankly owned that he was very deeply in love, mentioned his income, and earneftly implored her good opinion. He certainly knew which of the ladies he meant to addrefs, but being much agitated, and not very clear in his expreffions, he unhappily conveyed to her the arrogant hope that fhe was the objeĉt of his purfuit; fhe

K 3   therefore

therefore thanked him for the honour he had done her, but intreated him to defift from an addrefs which never could fucceed. Mr. Alfop defired fhe would confult her fifter, refufing to take a pofitive denial till Marianne was informed of his defign. Mifs Dudley thought this reference extraordinary, and told him her fifter's fentiments could make no change in her determination. Mr. Alfop anfwered, fhe was then very barbarous, and faid fomething about freedom, which Louifa miftaking, replied, fhe hoped freedom of opinion would be permitted to herfelf. At length the lover grew warm, and told her he faw her defigns, and was determined to overthrow them, and to carry his point, in fpite of all the oppofition fhe could make. Thus they feparated, the gentleman in furious indignation, and the lady wondering what fteps her refolute fwain would take, to compel her to attend him to the altar.

CHAP. XVII.

*A modern lover makes his exit, but not in a
style of high heroism.*

NO fooner was Mr. Alfop gone, than
Mifs Dudley, impelled (I fuppofe) by the
fpirit of envy, flew to her fifter, to inform
her of the ardent paffion fhe had infpired,
in a heart which Marianne certainly account-
ed her own. I cannot fay that the difpute
between the ladies was carried on with as
much acrimony as mirth; but certainly each
heroically complimented the other with offers to refign the contefted conqueft. Poor
Mr. Alfop's affair being foon difpatched, the
converfation turned upon the Clermonts.
Marianne commended the fimplicity, propriety, and modeft fweetnefs of the fifter;
and Louifa afked her, if fhe was not *now* a
convert to the brother's uncommon beauty ?
Marianne was refolutely determined againft
love: but, fince there was fuch a fimilarity
of foul, intended to cultivate a platonick

friend-

friendſhip with Mr. Clermont. I think in that heterogeneous compoſition beauty cannot be an eſſential quality. I rather ſuppoſe, ſince mind is the only objeĉt, it would ſubſiſt in its fulleſt perfeĉtion between old Blue Beard and Lady Meduſa. Marianne Dudley probably thought the ſame. She was ſhocked to hear her ſiſter talk of Mr. Clermont as merely an handſome man; while ſhe took no notice of that ſuperior virtue, that inherent excellence, that ſublime amiability which ſhe already diſcovered was congenial to his ſoul. Indeed Louiſa was apt to commend only what was apparent, and generally reſerved her praiſe of thoſe *latent* qualities, till their exiſtence was confirmed by experience.

Marianne paſſed the remainder of the day in peruſing paſtorals, and playing upon her harp. At night, after having taken leave of her ſiſter, Patty, with many apologies, many aſſurances that ſhe would not do ſuch a thing again for the world, many proteſta-

tions

tions that fhe met him quite by accident, and much pity beftowed upon the poor gentleman, put into her hand a billet-doux from Mr. Alfop. Marianne at firft declined reading it, till her fifter was prefent; but being affured by Patty that Mifs Dudley was not to know of it, ventured to break the feal. A love-letter is generally thought rather a difficult performance, and perhaps I fhall be of fervice to the rifing generation of fighing fwains if I communicate a warranted original:

' MADAM,

' As I have been certified by authentick testimony, that the party to whom I ftated my cafe is biaffed in judgment, and likely to hold back evidence, I have undertaken to plead my own caufe; and though I will not be fo bold as to afk a favourable verdict, depend upon receiving mercy. Firft, I premife, Madam, never was man more in love. Secondly, I could bring many witneffes to fpeak to my character. Third-

' ly,

' ly, I poffefs the fee-fimple of an eftate in
' the county of Weftmoreland, of feven
' hundred pounds per annum, devifed by my
' late father. Fourthly, I enjoy five thou-
' fand in the long annuities, by virtue of
' the will of my aunt Margaret Alfop, fpin-
' fter. Now, Madam, judge if I fhould be
' condemned unheard. Let the caufe come
' fpeedily to iffue, and believe me,

   ' Deareft of creatures,

    ' Yours till death,

     ' THOMAS ALSOP.

' N. B. Be pleafed to avoid naming this
fubject to Mifs Dudley.'

Though the humane Patty endeavoured
to excite her lady's compaffion for the mife-
rable writer, fhe was too much diverted by
the epiftle to attend for fome time to fentiments of pity. At length fhe inquired how
fhe could affift him, fince ftrictly prohibited
from faying any thing about him to her fifter, who was the perfon whofe favour he
was folicitous to obtain. This queftion
         brought

brought on an eclairciffement; Patty vow-
ing, that he protefted he was in love with
her lady, and Marianne as pofitively affirm-
ing that he had made propofals to Louifa
that very day. There is no arguing againft
facts. Patty was forced to give him up as a
bafe perjured lover, and deeply moralized'
upon the general infidelity of men, to exculpate herfelf from the charge of credulity,
in having been impofed upon by Mr. Alfop's pretended paffion. She received a pofitive injunction never to mention his name
to her miftrefs again, and to return his letter, with an intimation that his impertinence
would receive no other anfwer. Patty obey-
ed, and penned a furious epiftle; in which
fhe bitterly reproached him with having ex-
pofed her to her lady's refentment, and ruined his own hopes by his perfidious behaviour.

 Nothing could exceed the aftonifhment of
Mr. Alfop at this charge. Indeed the accufation of perfidy was extremely unjuft, as
ever

ever fince the firft encouraging ray beamed upon his love, he had been invariably fixed to the objeƌ of his purfuit; I mean the lovely Marianne's fortune. It was the objeƌ of his daily thoughts and nightly dreams; he had proceeded fo far as to plan the future method of expenditure. How then could he be falfe? Utterly ignorant of the name of the lady with whom he was charged with infidelity, he could only exclaim with Shake-fpear's Hero,

' That my aceufers know who have condemn'd me.'

In this agony he flew to receive the foft lenitives which friendfhip affords; but Captain Target thought proper to apply only corrofives to the wound. In pretty plain terms he called him a blundering fool, ornamenting his difcourfe with thofe flowers of rhetorick, which, though the repetition of them would be judged *difgraceful* to a female pen, are certainly efteemed by the gentlemen who ufe them as the very quinteffence of wit, and the

the criterion of manly fenfe. He at length
reluctantly confented to go to Stannadine,
and endeavour to difcover what this heinous
offence was. Indeed he was not in reality
forry at his friend's mifcarriage, having only
made ufe of him as a fkilful general does of
his raw, undifciplined troops, to difcover
the ftrength of the enemy previous to his ar-
ranging the grand attack; firmly perfuaded
that by a few of thofe fkilful manœuvres allowable in love as well as war, he could at
any time divert the laurel from Alfop's brows
to his own.

But if that hope had ever been well founded, "the golden glorious opportunity" was
loft. Mifs Marianne, dazzled by the attractive beams of friendfhip, not only refufed to look at love, but confidered it as a
falfe fire, and the fource of all female wretch-
ednefs.

Captain Target had the penetration to perceive this, and after joining in a hearty
laugh at his friend's miftake, prudently avoided

ed difcovering his own attachment; which
would indeed have banifhed him from the
enjoyment of Mr. Dudley's hofpitality, for
which he entertained a moft *profound* regard.

CHAP. XVIII.

Variety, an antidote to fatiety.

LOUISA informed her father of
the events which had happened in his abfence, and foon received from him the following anfwer:

'TO MISS DUDLEY.

  ' The playful vivacity with which my dear
' girl relates Affop's odd adventure, would
' lighten my bofom of many of its cares,
' were I not affured that your filial delicacy
' would induce you to conceal the affliction
' that rived your heart, and pretend to
' cheerfulnefs in the moment of agony; left
' you fhould reproach a confcience deeply
                                    ' wounded.

' wounded. I will not however increafe my
' real forrows by imaginary ones, but will
' fuppofe that I have not made my Louifa
' wretched.

'I rejoice from my very foul at Mari-
' anne's efcape : I will certainly wait upon
' Lord Clermont, to exprefs my gratitude
' to him and his fon, immediately upon my
' return. The intimacy he requefts will, I
' fear, be incompatible with the plans we
' muft too probably adopt. You tell me,
' unlefs a fifter's partiality deceives you, Mr.
' Clermont looks on Marianne with more
' than admiration. I fcarce wifh her to
' make a conqueft of fo *young* a lover.

' You exprefs a defire to hear of my own
' affairs. The only pleafant circumftances
' which have happened to me, have been
' owing to an accidental meeting with Mr.
' Pelham. As my connexions with Tonne-
' reau *muft* be divulged, I did not conceal
' from him the unpleafant motive of my
' journey. I am unable, Louifa, to exprefs
' the

' the manner in which this moſt excellent
' young man has endeavoured to confole
' me. He pofitively infifted that I fhould
' remove from the lodgings I had taken, and
' accept of an apartment in his houfe. He
' behaves to me with yet fuperior efteem and
' refpeft, than when he was at Stannadine
' foliciting your fifter's hand. Oh, that fhe
' had viewed him with approbation! we then
' fhould have enjoyed the comforts of pro-
' teftion, without feeling the miferies of de-
' pendance. But let us not repine: the
' events of life are guided by a wife direftor,
' who often extrafts real good out of feem-
' ing evil.

' Mr. Pelham has frequently mentioned
' you. He tells me Sir William Milton's
' attachment to you is more violent than
' ever, and that he is as wretched as pride,
' difappointment, and felf-reproach can make
' him. I find he has not been quite fo cri-
' minal as we conceived. The Mortons, my
' love, are artful women: the daughter, who

' is

' is uncommonly beautiful, was educated for
' the infamous purpofe of attracting the no-
' tice of fome man of fortune. She loft her
' character before fhe went to India, where,
' Mr. Pelham fays, fhe laid fuch fnares, as
' his coufin's prudence was unable to refift.
' You will be aftonifhed, but during the
' three years fhe lived with him, fhe made
' his lofty fpirit fubmit to what fhe pleafed
' to propofe. Mr. Pelham owns that fhe
' was at length left without any provifion,
' but this was not wholly her paramour's
' fault, as at their quarrelling fhe ftubbornly
' refufed to accept of any. Nothing was
' done for the children: this Mr. Pelham
' feverely reprobates; and I find has at
' length perfuaded Sir William to fettle one
' hundred a-year upon each of them.

 ' Lady Milton's health is rapidly declining.
' From the high character fhe had heard of
' you, fhe perfuaded herfelf you would foften
' thofe afperities in her fon's manner, which
' even a partial mother could not avoid per-
      ' ceiving.

' ceiving. Mr. Pelham is fo perfuaded that
' you are neceffary to Sir William's happi-
' nefs, that he wifhed me to fay whether I
' thought it poffible you could forgive the
' paft, if his future conduct fhould appear
' to deferve your efteem. I would not en-
' courage fuch a diftant expectation, or bind
' my Louifa to an improbable contingence.

' It is a pleafure to fee my amiable hoft in
' his own family : the regularity of his houfe-
' hold, the cheerful refpect of his fervants.
' He mingles in the world, but is not fafci-
' nated by its pleafures. His father's fifter
' lives with him; fhe does not feem remark-
' able either for her virtues or abilities; and
' I can perceive her temper is fomewhat in-
' jured by the infirmities of age: yet Mr.
' Pelham contrives to make every one as
' attentive to her as himfelf, and thus gives
' her an importance fhe would not otherwife
' poffefs. His behaviour proceeds from
' gratitude; for fhe nurfed him when an in-
' fant in a very dangerous illnefs; and it
' is

' is principally owing to her care that his life
' was prolonged. I live, my dear, in times
' when I hear much about publick virtue.
' Thofe actions of a man's life which are ex-
' hibited upon the theatre of the world are
' always of doubtful origin. Ambition and
' avarice may in reality claim what appears
' to proceed from patriotifm and benevo-
' lence; but the retired virtues of domeftick
' life are fure indications of that excellence
' of heart, and rectitude of intention, which
' the author of all good promifes to reward.

' Mr. Pelham never names your fifter: in
' this he is equally generous and delicate.
' He knows how my heart feconded his
' wifhes, and kindly avoids a fubject which
' could only give me pain. His active friend-
' fhip has difcovered a gleam of hope, which
' perhaps like many former ones will only
' end in deeper difappointment. An uncle
' of Mr. Tonnereau's, who died in Holland,
' bequeathed him an immenfe eftate. This
' was fuppofed to be placed beyond the
' reach

‘ reach of our Englifh laws; but an eminent
‘ counfellor, whofe opinion, unknown to
‘ me, Mr. Pelham has obtained, ftates, that
‘ he conceives it may be amenable to his
‘ debts; and I am advifed, as being the prin-
‘ cipal creditor, to attempt the recovery of
‘ it. My generous friend offers me every
‘ affiftance, and I fhall ftay fome time longer
‘ in London to hear further particulars.

‘ I will write to Marianne by this poft.
‘ She is a truly amiable child, and my af-
‘ fections are equally divided between my
‘ daughters; but the peculiar circumftances
‘ of my prefent fituation forbid me to dif-
‘ clofe to her my *whole* heart. My Louifa
‘ has long had a prefcriptive right to the
‘ confidence of her

‘ Affectionate father,

‘ RICHARD DUDLEY.

Such an epiftle could not but give delight
to a heart in which the flame of filial piety
glowed with pureft luftre: but perhaps it
was

was not wholly ascribable to that amiable quality, that Louisa, after pressing the letter to her lips, deposited it in her bosom, repeating at the same time her father's words, " that the author of all good would certainly reward the virtues of Mr. Pelham."

As Mr. Dudley's letter to Marianne is not essential to my design, I shall omit it. That young lady's apprehensions respecting her father's embarrassments had been considerably relieved, by the evasive answers of her sister; whose uniform cheerfulness, joined to the observation that the family arrangement was conducted in its usual liberal way, at length entirely removed the suspicion. Mrs. Patty too, who to serve a particular purpose had been the cause of exciting her alarm, perceiving that it did not take the right effect, took care to make Thomas unsay every hint, to the disadvantage of his master's fortune.

Marianne was now therefore *tolerably* easy; she never permitted herself to be more. Always dissatisfied with the present, regretting

regretting the paft, and anticipating the future, fhe became peculiarly ingenious in the
art of felf-tormenting. Her friendfhip for
Mr. Clermont (though only friendfhip) was
of fuch an apprehenfive kind, that it could
not promote the tranquillity of the bofom in
which it was cherifhed. It was fo peculiarly
fufceptible, that, notwithftanding his frequent vifits and marked attentions, it conti-
nually fuggefted the idea that fhe was not fo
amiable in his eye, as he was in her's. Thefe
reflections did not excite any alarm refpecting
the ftate of her heart; was it not fortified by
refolutions againft love? Befides, fhe recollected that in the beginning of their attachment fhe felt the fame doubts refpecting
the fincerity of her dear Eliza Milton.

The bar which had fubfifted to prevent
her confidential correfpondence with that
lady, during the period of Mr. Pelham's vifits, being removed, Mifs Milton had written
her a moft affectionate epiftle; in which,
though fhe lamented that the ill fuccefs of her
brother

brother and coufin had prevented the family
conne&ion fo much defired from taking
place, fhe obferved a bond ftill fubfifted,
more facred, more indiffoluble than any
other. She flourifhed a little upon the word
friendfhip, and then defired her deareft Marianne to remember its hallowed claims.
This produced a very diffufe reply, in which
fuch reafons were given for Mr. Pelham's
difmiffion, as entirely fatisfied the fair confident, who declared that her friend had a&-
ed with her ufual greatnefs of foul, in re-
je&ing a man whom (however unexceptionable) fhe could not love.

Marianne had now an additional employment, befides playing upon her harp, reading paftoral poetry, walking in the woods
by moonlight, and liftening to diftant waterfalls. She kept a journal of the events
of the day, and every morning difpatched
two fheets of paper, clofely written, to her
beloved Eliza. If any fceptical critick
fhould cenfure this as a violation of probabi-
lity,

lity, obferving that a lady leading a retired country life could not find matter for fuch voluminous details, I fhall pity his ignorance, and refer him to the produ&ion of many of my contemporaries; where he may be convinced, that fentiment is to the full as du&ile as gold, and when beaten thin will cover as incalculable an extent of furface.

END OF THE FIRST VOLUME.

LaVergne, TN USA
03 April 2011
222732LV00004B/121/P